THE ENTREPRENEUR'S GUIDE TO
THE
ART
OF
WAR

THE ENTREPRENEUR'S GUIDE TO

THE ART OF WAR

THE ORIGINAL CLASSIC TEXT INTERPRETED FOR THE MODERN BUSINESS WORLD

MARK SMITH

SIRIUS

SIRIUS

This edition published in 2022 by Sirius Publishing, a division of
Arcturus Publishing Limited,
26/27 Bickels Yard, 151–153 Bermondsey Street,
London SE1 3HA

ISBN: 978-1-3988-0237-7
AD007749UK

Printed in China

CONTENTS

INTRODUCTION

For more than two millennia, Sun Tzu's *The Art of War* has influenced the thinking of some of history's most successful decision-makers.

Originally scribed as a guide to achieving military victory while incurring minimal losses or – ideally – not fighting at all, it offers timeless lessons around strategy, tactics, the importance of wisdom and the marshalling of resources. It has been adopted in many spheres, from business and politics to sport and science.

Scholars believe the text was written by Sun Tzu, a general working for the Wu state in ancient China, but mystery still surrounds the exact year when *The Art of War* was written. Common consensus states it may have been between 475 and 221 BCE.

SUN TZU FOR BUSINESS

So how can an ancient text that talks of soldiers, sieges and sovereigns be translated for a business audience in the 21st century – and as an entrepreneur, why should you care?

After all, entrepreneurs are busy people.

They are usually time-poor and prefer to invest what little time they have in running and building their business. But consider what could be achieved by taking a step back and truly understanding the fundamental principles of strategy that underpin success.

Consider too how these timeless teachings can help you plan for success over the short, medium and longer term and help you to:

■ understand how to enter a new market;
■ outshine competitors;

- inspire the loyalty of your staff as well as the devotion of customers and clients;
- adapt to changing or even chaotic market conditions;
- develop long-term strategies for success.

All of these business principles and more are underpinned by exactly the same values as those taught by Sun Tzu all those years ago. So first let us look at the underlying principal tenets of Sun Tzu's *Art of War*, all of which are timeless and focus on several key, recurring themes.

AVOIDING CONFLICT

Perhaps the most important thing to understand before delving into what *The Art of War* is, is to understand first what it is not. *The Art of War* is not a call to arms which paints conflict as something to be glorified. Nor does it deal in-depth with how to deploy military tactics and equipment.

Indeed, one of the many unique aspects of Sun Tzu's philosophy is that, unlike many of the generals and masters of war who came before or who have followed since, he did not view conflict and combat as a route to glory.

Instead, he counselled avoiding military confrontation wherever possible and taught that the enemy could be vanquished before a single arrow was ever fired in anger. This was done by understanding yourself, your rivals and the wider situation. By doing so, you could plan your way to success.

Indeed, Sun Tzu believed that capturing the enemy's ground without waste or unnecessary effort or bloodshed was the only 'true' victory.

In a business context: victory with as little wasted time, effort and money is also your ultimate goal.

A SUCCESSFUL AND CONSIDERATE LEADER

Another theme the original text focuses on is the idea of leadership. At a time when glory and honour were intrinsically linked with the warrior mindset, it is difficult to overstate just what a radical break with conventional wisdom this was.

Throughout the teachings, one of the things that comes to the fore is the idea of the leader putting the success of the strategic objectives above their own personal glory and ambitions. In a business context, this leader is you.

THE LEADER'S ARMY

As is to be expected from a discourse on military strategy, the 'army' features heavily in the text. Sun Tzu discusses inspiring troops, promoting the right people to leadership roles, coordinating movement, inspiring loyalty and enforcing discipline. In business, this is your company. Even if you have no staff yet, the coordination of your business's operations is still an important part of what will make you a success.

THE ENEMY

Knowledge of the enemy was perhaps the most important aspect of a commander's ability to achieve victory, according to Sun Tzu. While many warriors of the era embraced hubris and raw aggression to overwhelm and defeat opponents, Sun Tzu taught that knowing an opponent as well as you know yourself provides a swifter, cleaner path to achieving objectives.

This knowledge could be gained via scouting, alliances, local guides and espionage. In a modern business context, this is your competitors.

THE WIDER SITUATION

Besides the leader's army and his opponent, there was also the wider situation to consider. This could include the weather, the land, and the extent to which factors beyond anyone's control could impact on the army's physical ability to move, as well as on the spirit of the soldiers and their opponent. In business, this is the market and the economy.

THE ENTREPRENEUR'S GUIDE TO *THE ART OF WAR*

In this book we will examine how Sun Tzu's teachings can be applied to modern business, illustrated by case studies involving some of the world's most famous companies. We will also hear from entrepreneurs as they share their own accumulated wisdom. From the educational technology sector in Singapore to the spice industry in the Republic of Ireland, and from Californian app developers to TED Talkers, you will find unique real-world examples, tips and insights that can help you on the road to success.

At the end of each chapter, you will find the original words of Sun Tzu upon which the chapter is based, offering you the opportunity to consider his advice for yourself.

CHAPTER 1

LAYING PLANS

The opening chapter to Sun Tzu's *The Art of War* concerned the importance of making preparations before engaging in military action. Indeed, this was arguably Sun Tzu's most important lesson – the idea that victory could effectively be secured during this phase of a campaign, before armies had even taken to the field.

The general who loses a battle makes but few calculations beforehand. Thus do many calculations lead to victory, and few calculations to defeat: how much more no calculation at all! It is by attention to this point that I can foresee who is likely to win or lose – *Sun Tzu*

PLANNING FOR SUCCESS

Laying plans is just as important for victory in business as it is in a military campaign. Whether it is having a clear vision and offering, written business plans, policies and procedures, social media and marketing strategies or having a unique selling point, the battle can be won or lost before the first product or service is ever taken to market.

When addressing the importance of planning, Sun Tzu spoke of what he called his five constant factors. Those who knew and embraced these five factors would be victorious and those who did not, would fail. The factors were:
■ the moral law;
■ Heaven;
■ Earth;

11

■ the commander;
■ method and discipline.

THE FIVE FACTORS FOR BUSINESS

So let us break down what these five factors mean and how they apply to business. The moral law is the willingness of people to follow their ruler. In a business context, this is the propensity of staff and employees to be fully onboard with the company's culture and goals.

What Sun Tzu termed 'Heaven' and 'Earth' are broadly related to the prevailing elemental and physical conditions of the battlefield. For Heaven, this was the seasons, night and day, cold and heat. Earth meant distances, open ground and narrow passes.

In business, this is broadly analogous to knowing the market. Is the market buoyant or depressed and is it seasonal in nature? What is the spending power of your typical customer or client? Is it a competitive market? Is it an old or new market and what is your competition like?

THE ENTREPRENEUR AS A LEADER

In this section, Sun Tzu also introduced the concept of the commander, something he would return to time and again in his text. In business, the commander is you. You are the entrepreneur, the person who takes the decisions, the owner, the leader, the dreamer and inspirer.

Sun Tzu said a good commander should be wise, sincere, benevolent and strict and have courage. They should also inspire trust. For someone to succeed in business it is important that they too inspire trust, not just in those that work with and for them – but in those they would do business with and sell to as well.

Most new businesses flow from the experiences of the founders. They see something, think it can be done better, and then have the guts to go off and do it – *Jeremy Stern*

One thing many entrepreneurs have in abundance is drive and self-belief. After all, they probably would not have taken on the challenge of starting a business in the first place if they did not have that burning inner fire.

That was certainly the case for Jeremy Stern. He had spent 20 years in the marketing industry, working with global powerhouses such as Unilever, and serving as head of European promotion for Coca-Cola and then European marketing director for the Japanese video game giant Sega. For Jeremy, it was while he was working for other companies and observing how things were done that the seeds of entrepreneurship were sown.

'I had seen that whilst there was huge senior focus on advertising with things like promotions, prize draws and competitions, they were left to the most junior person to organize. They had no idea of the rules, the risks and the need for compliance, and things frequently went wrong.'

It was at this point that he decided to shift the paradigm, so that the person at the top would be the one to take care of these types of requirements, providing hands-on and senior leadership where the clients and customers needed to see it most.

Small beginnings

In 2002, he set up shop in his back room, but from these humble beginnings things soon took off. His company PrimoVeritas now has 40 staff, in-house legal and web development teams, operates in more than 80 countries, runs over 1,500 projects a year and has long-term clients such as Pepsi, Walkers, ASOS, Amex and Kellogg's.

It is now the UK's leading promotional compliance specialists, which means it ensures that the prize draws, competitions and instant-win promotions operated by major food, drink, finance and other brands are run fairly, legally and securely.

The day-to-day aspect means the company drafts the terms and conditions for the offers we see in supermarkets, and also picks winners of prize draws and judges entries to competitions. Jeremy says: 'I decided there had to be a better someone who could take care of all of the details, make sure there were terms and conditions that the winners were picked fairly, that they were handled correctly and everything was legal, in the UK, in Europe, or beyond.'

THE IMPORTANCE OF YOU

Everything will eventually stem from the person at the top, so the most important thing is to find out what is unique about you as the entrepreneur.

What unique skills, insights, abilities or points of view do you bring to the table? What have you learned on your career journey that enables you to offer something different and do it better?

Being a capable and trustworthy leader will help you establish Sun Tzu's 'moral law', which will make staff, investors and external collaborators want to follow you and embrace your vision.

FIND YOUR NICHE

Sun Tzu talked of Heaven and Earth, the conditions in which the commander had to conduct his plans. In a business context, that represents the economy and markets, the business world through which you must navigate. This is something we will touch on in Chapters 4 and 7.

But in terms of entering a market, Stern's advice is that it is essential for the leader to set down their clear focus for what the company will do and how it will operate.

'Create a niche and stay in it. There are more than 10,000 creative marketing agencies in the UK. There are just two companies that do what we do.'

Although it might be tempting to diversify and go where you see bigger opportunities, the reality is that you will be competing with many more rivals, who may be better than you in areas outside of your core.

HONE YOUR EXPERTISE

Having a niche is something that many entrepreneurs are not sure about, as they instinctively feel they will be leaving money on the table from all the work that might pass them by.

But as well as helping to establish you as a business with fewer competitors, it has the considerable added bonus of ensuring you are immersed in a subject and a sector, providing you with invaluable specialist expertise that is evolving all the time – expertise which will command a value, possibly a high value.

Jeremy said that sticking to this core offering and becoming experts in a field means business will eventually flow to you. Once they are customers, this opens the door to diversifying an offering to that specific client which can lead to even more business. This is something PromoVeritas did successfully.

'When you get that business, then it is possible to "add on" extra bits. In our case, prize buying, prize fulfilment, web building, but it is a bolt-on for the service that makes us special – legal work on promotions and fair winner selection.'

SETTING THE RULES

Finally, in Sun Tzu's list of the five factors, method and discipline are all about organization:

■ How is your business structured?
■ Who does what?
■ How efficiently does it interact with the market, suppliers and customers?
■ How disciplined is the company with expenditure?

Establishing and nurturing relationships with suppliers and routes to market is every bit as important for a business as it is for an army to maintain its supply lines on the battlefield.

The methods for opening these routes, such as negotiating with potential suppliers, right down to attending trade fares and breakfast meetings at local business organizations, are wide and varied.

Discipline in a financial sense is crucial too. Just as Sun Tzu knew that an army relied on gold to keep it stocked and supplied, so must a business operate within its means. Remaining financially solvent and being able to successfully weigh risk vs reward will be one of the main factors that decides whether a business survives, grows, and thrives. This is also something we will touch on in greater detail later (see page 57).

PREPARING TO MOVE

The very essence of what Sun Tzu taught was the idea that everything should be structured, thought out and planned before any actual physical actions were taken. Indeed, it was at this stage – not the actual exchanging of strikes and counterstrikes – where the war was won and lost. The same is true of business.

Many an entrepreneur has fallen foul of moving before they were ready, whether it was launching the business itself or trying to secure new markets before a product was up and running properly.

SHATTERED GLASS

Even the biggest and most experienced companies in the world are not immune to failure. In 2013, hopes were high in an excited tech sector when search engine giant Google launched Google Glass. This was a product breaking new ground and ushering in an exciting era of wearable technology.

In theory, at least. But things did not quite work out that way.

The technology did not go down well. The notion of spectacles that could record everything and provide information in real time just did not seem to capture the public's imagination, and Google Glass has been synonymous with the phrase 'business flop' ever since.

A company with almost immeasurable resources and a reputation as an efficient and innovative global powerhouse had tried something new, seemingly not equipped with the right understanding of what the consumer wanted, and it failed spectacularly.

LAYING SOLID FOUNDATIONS

If a wealthy giant like Google is no stranger to setbacks, then the stakes are even higher for smaller companies. To offer just one unfortunate statistic: in 2019, the failure rate of start-ups was around 90 per cent, with one in five failing in the first year. But one start-up that has not only survived but flourished is the food-sharing app Olio.

The company was founded by Saasha Celestial-One and her business partner Tessa Clarke back in 2015. It has since grown from a local initiative in north London to a company with a presence in 51 countries and more than two million users.

The daughter of Iowa hippy entrepreneurs (hence the origin of the last name, Celestial-One – which her parents made up), Saasha grew up in a large, relatively poor family. She spent much of her childhood accompanying her mother on missions to rescue things that others had discarded – wooden fixtures and fittings from foreclosed houses, plants from the greenhouse dumpster and aluminium soda cans (worth 5¢ each) casually tossed aside at the beach.

The two women met doing their MBAs. Before that, each had honed their business skills at the world's biggest companies – Tessa working for Boston Consulting Group, and Saasha at McKinsey.

With that kind of background, it stood to reason that they were not going to jump into a new market without doing their homework first.

Before even launching their company, they realized how important it was to conduct thorough research. 'Tessa and I were immediately convinced that we were on to something which could be huge, but we had to rein ourselves in a bit,' says Saasha. 'The first step was to validate the total available market (TAM) – we knew we hated wasting food, or waste of any kind, but just how big of a problem was it?'

There is a variety of ways to calculate total available market, also known as total addressable market. These include:

■ top-down;
■ bottom-up;
■ value theory.

1. Top down:

Top-down analysis looks at an entire industry and attempts to drill down into where your business could play a part and, hopefully, make some money. This technique employs the use of resources such as industry reports and research to build a picture of the size of the market as well as its major players. Typically, it is a case of researching reports and assessing data such as 'the coffee industry in France is worth xxx and increased by x per cent in the last five years'.

While much easier and less time-consuming to undertake than other methods, a potential issue is that it relies on third-party information.

Also, while you are trying to assess your potential for seizing market share, this method also does not take into account whether your product is disruptive. By disruptive, I mean that your idea is a radical departure from what is already out there – for example, a whole new type of coffee. If it is disruptive, it may not be constrained by the same rules as the other players already doing business in that market. We will talk about disruption later (see page 90).

2. Bottom up:

Bottom-up analysis uses your own early experiences in the market to see how things might pan out further down the line if you choose to expand. This is considered more accurate because it uses your own experience and data to fill in the blanks, rather than macro data encompassing an entire market as used in top-down analysis.

To use the coffee analysis, this could be a case of: 'I've sold 500 cups of coffee a day with one store, if I were to have 50 stores nationwide that would be 500×50 a day = 25,000 cups.'

The downside here is that your relatively narrow experience may not translate nationally and may not be able to anticipate the nuances that can impact success or failure. For instance, have you built up a loyal following? Do you have fewer competitors than you might encounter in other towns and cities? Is the customer base significantly different due to socio-economic factors, the presence of universities, etc?

3. Value theory:

Unlike the other two methods, there is less maths at work here and more educated guesswork. This is about assessing how much value your product or service can add to the market and is especially useful when you are treading new ground in a young market where statistics and reports may be in short supply.

For example, when Netflix launched its streaming model, it had no major competitors except for the DVD industry. Conducting top-down or bottom-up research may not have helped in that situation because there was nothing like it around it the time.

In this type of situation, a company would have to assess what value there was to a totally new way of viewing films at home. How could it add value to the consumer by providing a completely online library and replacing physical disks? This type of analysis can be particularly useful for tech start-ups and disruptive companies that are especially ground-breaking and unique.

FINDING VALUE FOR OLIO

When they set out to conduct their analysis of the market, Tessa and Saasha's research revealed there was a massive need for their new food waste app. Saasha said: 'We were absolutely shocked to discover that over a third of all food produced is never eaten, a loss of over $1 trillion per year. We figured if we could unlock even a fraction of that lost value, we'd be in business.'

The duo put together a market research survey using the SurveyMonkey website and shared the link online via local Facebook groups. One thing to note here for anyone just starting out is that both of these methods are free. They received 350 responses, which they felt was a high enough total for the results to be statistically meaningful. In the survey, 35 per cent of respondents said they felt 'physically pained' throwing away food that is – or was recently – edible, and over 90 per cent of people said they would walk 10–15 minutes to collect homegrown food from a neighbour.

Make sure you don't only research people who are likely to give you the answer you want – *Saasha Celestial-One*

Saasha and Tessa selected 12 people from the survey who all said they were 'really excited' about the proposal in their responses and who lived close to each other but did not know each other, and the asked them to take part, along with one local business which had also shown support. 'We put the 13 participants in a WhatsApp group and the rules were simple. Over 14 days, share any spare food, and if you want an item, message to request it. In under an hour we had the first share – a bag of shallots! We were ecstatic! We watched with bated breath as over the next 14 days 26 shares took place.

'At the end of the proof of concept, we debriefed with all of the users. This was incredibly insightful as we learned that many of the features we thought were essential to Version 1 of the app, such as user ratings and a map, were not.'

Armed with this research they were able to use these insights to strip back the core version of their app and launch sooner. In the end it was only five months from forming Olio to launching in the App Store, followed by Google Play three weeks later.

GET TO KNOW YOUR NEW CUSTOMERS
Your customers are out there; they just do not know it yet. When you are trying to seize your share of a market, you can give yourself an advantage by drilling down into what consumers in your chosen market really want. It is this attention to detail that has seen Saasha and Tessa's app take off so quickly.

Saasha says: 'My advice to my fellow entrepreneurs is to make sure you don't only research people who are likely to give you the answer you want.

'For example, at Olio when researching different product features, we survey transactional users, dormant users, and – most importantly – people who aren't users yet at all.

'Also, make sure you research both via survey to get a large sample and via user interviews to go deep.

'Use an interview guide and have two people on present for the interview, one to take verbatim notes and one to facilitate and probe.'

FINDING YOUR PLACE IN THE MARKET

Arun Kapil co-founded Green Saffron at the height of the credit crunch when the odds were stacked against him.

Since those early days back in 2007, the Anglo-Indian chef, who is based in the Republic of Ireland, has turned the company into a multi-award-winning purveyor of spices, rice, sauces and spice blends.

Starting with just a market stall with one person helping out, he grew the business and said constant innovation was key to making the most of the opportunities that presented themselves.

Since then, both Green Saffron and Arun himself have enjoyed huge success. He regularly appears on Ireland's Virgin Media, where he has a cookery segment on *The 6 O'Clock Show*, along with appearances on Channel 4's *Sunday Brunch* and regular appearances on RTE's *Today Show*. He has also appeared as a 'leading spice industry expert' on the BBC's *MasterChef*.

For Arun, getting to know the market he was moving into was an essential component of laying plans. It was also important not simply to replicate what was already out there but to bring something different. 'Firstly, you need to get the basics right and make sure you have all the intel you can gather on your target market from conventionally available reports and through your own observations.'

ACCESSING LOCAL SUPPORT

Arun could harness the support available in Ireland when he was initially doing research. 'We're fortunate here in Ireland to have such a great resource provided by our food board, Bord Bia. Support is available in many forms from local enterprise boards, to your own network to the proliferation of new companies that are increasingly popping-up.'

INTELLIGENT ANALYSIS

It was Clive Humby, the British mathematician and architect of the Tesco Clubcard for one of the UK's biggest supermarkets, who once said: 'Data is the new oil'. Indeed, there is more information available than ever, about customer behaviour, their likes and dislikes, spending power, how they buy (in person, online or on their phones) and how likely they are to become a customer – and stay a customer.

Any company looking to gain a foothold in a new market would be looking a digital gift horse in the mouth by not at least considering what data analytics services are out there.

Arun says: 'Data capture and having a good grasp on your target market is a must.

'The number of artificial intelligence "data sweeper" providers that now exist are taking away the traditional need to have such deep pockets to afford the vast sums often demanded for data by the established houses.

'This is a good thing. The new artificial intelligence companies are there for the challenger as well as the established. Seek out the best fit for you.

'Ultimately, I am a firm believer in "boots on the ground" intelligence. If you can collaborate with a trusted local resource, you stand a chance of circumventing a lot of heartache.'

Once your research is done – and before getting ready to move, he suggests the following:

- Make sure your offering is the best it can be and that you have positive research data from trials to show it.
- Make sure your idea answers a need of your target audience and that you are able to show your audience that the need actually does exist.
- Do not just sell the product to the customer, but sell the way that your product can be sold to the consumer as well.
- Keep all communication simple, clear and concise – and present your idea or product in its best way, which is most accessible to your target market.

CONCLUSIONS

When Sun Tzu spoke about laying plans. he talked of the five factors: the moral law, Heaven and Earth, the commander, method and discipline.

All of these factors related to how best you could prepare for your great adventure, whether it be the conquest of a land or, indeed, a market. When condensed, these principles centre around the importance of the leader and of understanding what lies ahead.

From a business perspective, these are the relevant lessons for us to bear in mind:

■ Challenge yourself to be an inspiring leader.

■ Everything stems from you as the entrepreneur. You must be clear on your vision if you are to inspire not just your employees and teammates, but anyone who is to do business with you or give you their custom.

■ Never forget the importance of research.

■ Whether it is interviews, surveys, bringing in advanced data analytics, or simply talking to people, you must have the right data to determine whether or not there is a need for the service you are planning to provide or the product you hope to sell.

Laying Plans

(Sun Tzu's Original Text)

1. Sun Tzu said: The art of war is of vital importance to the State.

2. It is a matter of life and death, a road either to safety or to ruin. Hence it is a subject of inquiry which can on no account be neglected.

3. The art of war, then, is governed by five constant factors, to be taken into account in one's deliberations, when seeking to determine the conditions obtaining in the field.

4. These are:
   (1) The Moral Law;
   (2) Heaven;
   (3) Earth;
   (4) The Commander;
   (5) Method and Discipline.

5 & 6.   The Moral Law causes the people to be in complete accord with their ruler, so that they will follow him regardless of their lives, undismayed by any danger.

7.   Heaven signifies night and day, cold and heat, times and seasons.

8.   Earth comprises distances, great and small; danger and security; open ground and narrow passes; the chances of life and death.

9.   The Commander stands for the virtues of wisdom, sincerity, benevolence, courage and strictness.

10.   By Method and Discipline are to be understood the marshalling of the army in its proper subdivisions, the graduations of rank among the officers, the maintenance of roads by which supplies may reach the army, and the control of military expenditure.

11.   These five heads should be familiar to every general: he who knows them will be victorious; he who knows them not will fail.

12.   Therefore, in your deliberations, when seeking to determine the military conditions, let them be made the basis of a comparison, in this wise:—

13. (1) Which of the two sovereigns is imbued with the Moral Law?
(2) Which of the two generals has most ability?
(3) With whom lie the advantages derived from Heaven and Earth?
(4) On which side is Discipline most rigorously enforced?
(5) Which army is stronger?
(6) On which side are officers and men more highly trained?
(7) In which army is there the greater constancy both in reward and punishment?

14. By means of these seven considerations I can forecast victory or defeat.

15. The general that hearkens to my counsel and acts upon it, will conquer: let such a one be retained in command! The general that hearkens not to my counsel nor acts upon it, will suffer defeat:— let such a one be dismissed!

16. While heeding the profit of my counsel, avail yourself also of any helpful circumstances over and beyond the ordinary rules.

17. According as circumstances are favourable, one should modify one's plans.

18. All warfare is based on deception.

19. Hence, when able to attack, we must seem unable; when using our forces, we must seem inactive; when we are near, we must make the enemy believe we are far away; when far away, we must make him believe we are near.

20. Hold out baits to entice the enemy. Feign disorder, and crush him.

21. If he is secure at all points, be prepared for him. If he is in superior strength, evade him.

22. If your opponent is of choleric temper, seek to irritate him. Pretend to be weak, that he may grow arrogant.

23. If he is taking his ease, give him no rest. If his forces are united, separate them.

24. Attack him where he is unprepared, appear where you are not expected.

25. These military devices, leading to victory, must not be divulged beforehand.

26. Now the general who wins a battle makes many calculations in his temple ere the battle is fought. The general who loses a battle makes but few calculations beforehand. Thus do many calculations lead to victory, and few calculations to defeat: how much more no calculation at all! It is by attention to this point that I can foresee who is likely to win or lose.

CHAPTER 2

WAGING WAR

When Sun Tzu writes about the art of waging war, it is here that we start to get a feel for just how different a military mind he had compared to other commanders. This chapter is notable for its lack of discussion of military tactics such as the use of archers or cavalry, and its focus instead on practical issues such as supplies, money and motivating the army.

The importance of winning with minimum delay was crucial to Sun Tzu's military thinking, for he feared that the longer a conflict endured, the more the army would start to flounder and the more the money needed to fund the war would dry up.

This was a remarkable insight for a commander during that era – the insight that armies were composed of people with hopes and fears who succumbed to tiredness and lost hope, rather than being warriors bound by notions of honour and duty, who felt both prepared and obliged to fight to the death for the glory of their leader.

When you engage in actual fighting, if victory is long in coming, then men's weapons will grow dull and their ardour will be damped.

As well as the impact of protracted conflict on the performance of an army, Sun Tzu also cautioned against the impact on finances too:

'Again, if the campaign is protracted, the resources of the State will not be equal to the strain.'

What's more, armies had to be fed and supplied. With this in mind, he advocated the idea of ensuring an army not only had enough supplies before it set out, but was also prepared to forage when required: 'Bring war material with you from home, but forage on the enemy. Thus the army will have food enough for its needs.'

WAR AND BUSINESS

The word 'war' may not lend itself to what most entrepreneurs consider to be part of their everyday lives in business, but in many ways, there are a lot of similarities between business and war.

Wars feature different sides trying to achieve a military objective. Business features competitors trying to secure market share for their service or product.

Both endeavours require planning, strategy, marshalling of resources, knowing the lay of the land and the opponent well, and having adequate resources and manpower to achieve the goal.

FINDING A COMPETITIVE EDGE

In a free-market economy, business is fiercely competitive. Indeed, there are strong rules and regulations enacted and enforced to ensure this remains the case.

In essence, 'war' in a business context is encouraged because the theory holds that competition results in businesses refining their operations, their competitiveness also producing better services or more desirable products for the customer.

Well, that's the theory. But with only a finite number of customers in any field, each entrepreneur must do battle to seize and maintain their market share.

Something Sun Tzu fiercely believed in when it came to achieving victory was the idea of speed – being swift and seizing opportunities quickly.

He also states: 'Thus, though we have heard of stupid haste in war, cleverness has never been associated with long delays.'

The key to knowing the difference between being too hasty, while also knowing when you should avoid unnecessary delay, is to ask yourself if you are adequately prepared for the endeavour you are about to embark on.

If you plan to enter a market with a new product or service, is the speed with which you are doing so compromising any aspect of that product or service's chances of success?

Are you cutting corners? Or are you simply delaying because you want every single aspect of your new venture to be 'perfect'? Something which arguably can never be achieved.

If you are cutting corners, for example, because your product is not fully ready for market or your marketing plan is not fully executable, this could compromise your chances of success and in this instance, this would be haste rather than speed.

But, if the only thing stopping you from taking swift action is a worry or concern that will have no tangible impact on the potential success of what you're doing, then that could constitute an unnecessary delay.

Ask yourself: 'If I could press fast forward on what I'm doing now, would it increase my chance of failure?'

If the answer is no, then you are not being hasty, you are simply being smart in avoiding an unnecessary delay.

A NEW PLAYER

One company that famously seized its market share swiftly, and with a clear plan of attack, was Virgin Atlantic.

Entering a marketplace often virtually monopolized by state-run enterprises such as British Airways, Virgin Atlantic was established by Alan Hellary, Richard Branson and Randolph Fields and championed the idea of 'putting the customer first'.

Having started life as the brainchild of Anglo-US lawyer Randolph Fields, the company wasted no time in taking on its more established competitors. Instead of arrows and chariots, its weapon was the clear vision and passion of its founders, with the desire for an expedient entry into the market at its core. Branson's declared approach to business was either to succeed within the first year or to exit the market. He was also undeterred by fear of failure:

It is only through failure that we learn. Many of the world's finest minds have learned this the hard way – Sir Richard Branson

SWIFT SUCCESSES

Launched in 1984, Virgin Atlantic had leased its first planes within only three months and set up an operation from the UK to the USA.

It quickly expanded its first transatlantic routes to include Miami, Orlando, New York, Los Angeles and Boston.

What followed were new global routes, including Hong Kong, Athens and Tokyo. The firm relentlessly introduced a string of firsts as it waged its assault on British Airways' market share, including in-flight entertainment and individual TV screens for passengers, and introducing complimentary, chauffeur-driven cars from the airport, drive-thru check in services, beds and in-flight beauty therapists.

Branson has said that when they set out to create Virgin Atlantic, he was trying to create the perfect airline for himself. It was this passion, coupled with the frustration of what he felt was missing in the industry, that drove the company's early successes.

Branson was up against a powerful, state-run operator whose finances and resources he could not at that time hope to match, but that did not matter.

Entrepreneurship is a great leveller. The wonderful thing is that money is not the sole currency when it comes to

starting a business; drive, determination, passion and hard work are all free and more valuable than a pot of cash
– Sir Richard Branson.

REWARDING YOUR TROOPS

Another vital aspect of waging war, about which both Sun Tzu and Branson would probably have agreed, is the need to motivate your forces.

Sun Tzu said soldiers should be rewarded for going above and beyond on the battlefield, with a successful commander knowing how to encourage them and incentivize them in the field. 'That there may be advantage from defeating the enemy, they must have their rewards.'

'Therefore in chariot fighting, when ten or more chariots are taken, those should be rewarded who took the first.'

Branson too has strongly advocated rewarding and incentivizing staff. In fact, for a company that endeavoured to seize part of the market from major players like British Airways by championing customer experience, Branson has admitted that a crucial part of creating customer experience was first looking after those who look after the customers – namely Virgin's employees.

I have always believed that the way you treat
your employees is the way you will treat your customers
and that people flourish when they are praised
– Sir Richard Branson

The company introduced a range of incentives for staff, ranging from staff travel and private health insurance, to gym memberships and festival tickets. When Branson's airline won $945,000 from a lawsuit against British Airways in 1993, he divided the money between his employees as a Christmas bonus.

Ensuring staff get their share of rewards from a company's growth and success is something Arun also agrees on.

'Hard work and tangible achievements should always be rewarded.

'This can be as simple as praise through to toasting with a glass or two, to night outs or financial bonus.

'Whatever form the reward takes, it is important to recognize the good, and to take a breath to recognize achievements. These are, after all, the milestones on the road to reaching your vision and it's important to reflect on them.'

Like many entrepreneurs, he says that stopping to acknowledge success was not always his strong point because he was always thinking about the 'next challenge'.

Some words of wisdom from his dad taught him to take a step back and appreciate things.

'This is something I have never been very good at, always wanting to keep moving on apace, not looking back.

'My father probably put it best; it's important to make sure you take time to review "the things".'

MAKING YOUR RESOURCES GO FURTHER

Sun Tzu warned against the idea of protracted conflicts that put a heavy strain on the state's resources, but he also advocated the idea of foraging in enemy territory. The ability to keep costs in line and to make do and mend when the need arises are two extremely valuable weapons in an entrepreneur's armoury.

THE STRATEGY OF COST REDUCTION

Carla Williams Johnson is a marketing and advertising strategist based in Trinidad and Tobago in the Caribbean. With more than 15 years in the industry, she has worked with global clients such as Coca-Cola, Unilever and Nestlé.

For Carla, keeping costs in line to ensure longevity has been all about thinking long term.

'This really comes down to strategy. You really need to know your end goal and have a strategic plan to get there. Having this will help you understand exactly where you need to invest your time, energy and money so you're not all over the place spending on things that won't give you any returns.'

Carla advises having at least a six-month plan of what you want to achieve, then mapping out what systems or experts you will need to achieve these goals. 'This will give a clear indication of where to truly spend your hard-earned money.'

ESTABLISHING A FINANCIAL STRATEGY

There is no exhaustive, one-size-fits-all methodology for building a financial methodology, but there are some common factors that will enable you to monitor costs.

A financial strategy should take into account:
- What position is your company in now?
- Where do you want it to be?
- How are you going to get there?

It should also take into account:
- How will you fund your future plans?
- What is your current expenditure?
- What is your current business model?
- What sources of finance are open to you (loans, savings, potential investors, etc)?

But while financial planning is important, there are also practical things an entrepreneur can do to make cash and resources stretch further too.

ESSENTIAL OR 'NICE TO HAVE'?

Olio is a company founded on a deep dislike of waste, and its founders were eager to keep things lean right from the start. With 40 full-time staff, they chose to become a remote working company from Day

One, which has helped keep costs down.

Saasha has kitted out her entire workspace with gear from the charitable recycling network FreeCycle.

'Tessa and I are both mums, and participating in the day-to-day with our children has always been important.

'I'd advise other entrepreneurs to ask themselves at every budget approval: will this move the needle for my business or is it a "nice to have"?

'If not, try to find a free way to go about getting to the same result.'

CONCLUSIONS

Sun Tzu strongly advocated the idea of swift success when it came to achieving goals. He cautioned against the impact of protracted campaigns and also said it was important to share the spoils of success to help motivate an army.

Keeping costs down and foraging from an enemy when possible were also key, enabling the army to survive longer in the field.

■ From a business perspective, these are the relevant lessons for us to bear in mind.

■ Be swift and decisive.

■ Once your plans are in place (see Chapter 1), you should be quick in pursuing your goals. Dithering can lead to greater expense and you will either succeed, or not.

■ Share the spoils.

■ If you are successful, share the fruits of your success with your employees. This could take many forms, from financial benefits to simply showing gratitude.

■ Be mindful of costs.

■ Ensure you are always mindful of costs. Have a financial strategy and keep expenses down where you can.

Waging War

(Sun Tzu's Original Text)

1.   Sun Tzu said: In the operations of war, where there are in the field a thousand swift chariots, as many heavy chariots, and a hundred thousand mail-clad soldiers, with provisions enough to carry them a thousand *li*[1], the expenditure at home and at the front, including entertainment of guests, small items such as glue and paint, and sums spent on chariots and armour, will reach the total of a thousand ounces of silver per day. Such is the cost of raising an army of 100,000 men.

2.   When you engage in actual fighting, if victory is long in coming, then men's weapons will grow dull and their ardour will be damped. If you lay siege to a town, you will exhaust your strength.

3.   Again, if the campaign is protracted, the resources of the State will not be equal to the strain.

4.   Now, when your weapons are dulled, your ardour damped, your strength exhausted and your treasure spent, other chieftains will spring up to take advantage of your extremity. Then no man, however wise, will be able to avert the consequences that must ensue.

---

1   One *li* is equal to half a kilometre.

5. Thus, though we have heard of stupid haste in war, cleverness has never been seen associated with long delays.

6. There is no instance of a country having benefited from prolonged warfare.

7. It is only one who is thoroughly acquainted with the evils of war that can thoroughly understand the profitable way of carrying it on.

8. The skilful soldier does not raise a second levy, neither are his supply-wagons loaded more than twice.

9. Bring war material with you from home, but forage on the enemy. Thus the army will have food enough for its needs.

10. Poverty of the State Exchequer causes an army to be maintained by contributions from a distance. Contributing to maintain an army at a distance causes the people to be impoverished.

11. On the other hand, the proximity of an army causes prices to go up; and high prices cause the people's substance to be drained away.

12. When their substance is drained away, the peasantry will be afflicted by heavy exactions.

13 & 14. With this loss of substance and exhaustion of strength, the homes of the people will be stripped bare, and three-tenths of their income will be dissipated; while government expenses for broken chariots, worn-out horses, breast-plates and helmets, bows and arrows, spears and shields, protective mantles, draught-oxen and heavy wagons, will amount to four-tenths of its total revenue.

15. Hence a wise general makes a point of foraging on the enemy. One cartload of the enemy's provisions is equivalent to twenty of one's own, and likewise a single *picul*[2] of his provender is equivalent to twenty from one's own store.

16. Now in order to kill the enemy, our men must be roused to anger; that there may be advantage from defeating the enemy, they must have their rewards.

17. Therefore in chariot fighting, when ten or more chariots have been taken, those should be rewarded who took the first. Our own flags should be substituted for those of the enemy, and the chariots mingled and used in conjunction with ours. The captured soldiers should be kindly treated and kept.

18. This is called using the conquered foe to augment one's own strength.

19. In war, then, let your great object be victory, not lengthy campaigns.

20. Thus it may be known that the leader of armies is the arbiter of the people's fate, the man on whom it depends whether the nation shall be in peace or in peril.

---

2 One *picul* weighs approximately 133 lbs.

CHAPTER 3

ATTACK BY STRATAGEM

In this chapter of *The Art of War*, Sun Tzu introduced several diverse concepts designed to enable a commander to achieve their military goals.

Firstly, it is important to note that the word stratagem is not the same as strategy. The latter refers to a broad long-term goal or set of goals while a stratagem is a self-contained plan, usually involving an element of deception.

Indeed, the idea of mounting unconventional attacks is a recurring theme throughout Sun Tzu's work. From the use of spies and deception to employing local guides and pretending to be weak when you are strong, or strong when you are weak – all can be useful tools in achieving victory without the need for brute force.

As well as the importance of capturing targets intact, he also revisits the concept of the relationship between a leader and the army and the ways in which a leader could undermine that army's success. It is in this chapter too that we read what is perhaps Sun Tzu's most famous quotation:

If you know the enemy and know yourself, you need not fear the result of a hundred battles. If you know yourself but not the enemy, for every victory gained you will also suffer a defeat. If you know neither the enemy nor yourself, you will succumb in every battle.

TAKING A TARGET INTACT

This chapter is also where Sun Tzu introduces the importance of achieving military objectives without destroying what the commander hoped to capture.

In the practical art of war, the best thing of all is to take the enemy's country whole and intact; to shatter and destroy it is no good. So too, it is better to recapture an army entire than to destroy it.

As we have noted already, Sun Tzu was a pragmatist. He viewed war as an endeavour designed not to bring honour or glory, but to achieve specific goals.

For him, destroying a target rather than capturing it intact made the whole enterprise utterly futile.

MARKET SHARE

As an army's objective may be to capture a city or a country, so a business's objective is to capture a market – or at least part of it. This is its market share.

Market share refers to your company's total sales in relation to the overall sales in that industry.

Whether a company is entering a new market and wants to capture a share, or whether it is attempting to solidify or expand its share in a market where it already does business, there are various ways it can achieve these goals.

These can include:
- Innovating;
- Creating a new product or putting a unique twist on an existing one;
- Dropping prices;
- Lowering prices to undercut the competition;
- Strengthening existing relationships with customers;
- If you have an existing customer base, you can target them for greater sales with promotions such as loyalty schemes;
- Advertising;
- A good advertising strategy is a great way to increase brand awareness. This is something we will touch on later;
- Improving product quality;
- You may not have created a new product, but you can increase the quality of something that is already out there;
- Acquiring a competitor;
- Purchasing a rival gives you a ready-made greater slice of your market and also has the additional benefit of removing them as a competitor on the playing field.

DANGERS OF DAMAGING THE MARKET

As Sun Tzu warned against the notion of the army completely destroying a country it was trying to capture, so too is there the danger of a company destroying a market from which it is trying to capture a share.

Companies that choose to lower prices can put their competitors out of business, but that also lowers the cost expectations of customers which can be like shooting yourself in the foot.

A firm may then find itself in a situation where it has no or few competitors but cannot turn a profit. A pointless exercise, Sun Tzu would surely say.

BEWARE THE RACE TO THE BOTTOM

Stephanie Scheller is the founder of Grow Disrupt, a San Antonio-based training organization for small businesses, and a speaker.

She has worked behind the scenes with more than 2,500 companies in the past five years to analyze and address their sales, marketing and methods of doing business. She is a TEDx speaker, a Forbes 30 under 30 nominee, a 2019 New York Life Woman of the Year Nominee and a two-time bestselling author.

'I don't recommend dropping your rates to get market share as a small business. You can't beat the major competitors on price and it's a terrible race to the bottom. It's usually a great way to destroy your brand,' she says.

'One major challenge you can run into when entering a new market is that you could find yourself flooding a market that is already saturated and damaging the market, driving other businesses (including yourself!) out of the market.

'Not to mention, you can severely damage your own business by overextending yourself financially, or dilute your brand so no one knows what you stand for anymore and your sales can drop.

'You could also overextend your team with the same results.'

TAKE TIME TO EVALUATE

Instead of rushing in and doing whatever it takes to achieve a foothold, Stephanie says careful planning is key. She advocates taking time to evaluate what is working and, just as importantly, what is not working in that market currently.

'Find a way to stand out by solving a problem that few of your competition has solved. Have a new product or a service that you are offering that stands out.

'For example, if your marketplace hates the buying process because it's complicated and manipulative, find a way to simplify it like Carvana did when they made an all-online-shopping process for car purchasing.'

LEVERAGE YOUR EXISTING GOOD NAME

Perhaps you have achieved success in one market and want to enter a new one? In these circumstances you do not necessarily have to begin from scratch.

Stephanie adds that when you have an existing market in which you are already known, there is nothing to stop you leveraging the success and reputational excellence you have already gained there, even if the market you have chosen to enter now is completely different.

'When you enter the market, lean on your previously established brand – when appropriate – to build trust with your audience.'

BE CAREFUL WITH PRICING

Cost and value are two very different things. The cost is the price, nothing more and nothing less. Value can mean many different things to many different people depending on what their needs are at any given time.

ADDING VALUE IS PRICELESS

From that perspective, careful pricing was something that has played a major part in helping to make Jeremy Stern's company PromoVeritas such a success.

By its very nature, it was a trailblazer in a new market, so there was virtually no precedent for how they would go about charging for their services when they first launched.

'It soon became clear that the type of service that we were offering was seen by clients to be more akin to professional lawyers, and by comparison, our fees were remarkably good value.

'But in addition, whilst we would base fees on an estimate of hours to be spent, if we said X hours, and it was actually X plus 10 hours, we did not charge the client more.

'Having been a client, I knew how their budgets worked and seeking more money at the end of a project is a complete pain. So fixed pricing was hugely reassuring to most of our clients and led to us getting more work and if necessary, for the next one, we would explain the overage and agree a bit more on that next project.'

A COMMANDER AND THEIR ARMY

In implementing a stratagem, Sun Tzu warned in *The Art of War* there were many ways in which a leader could stifle the prospects of victory.

These were:

■ By commanding the army to advance or to retreat, being ignorant of the fact that it cannot obey. This is called hobbling the army.

■ By attempting to govern an army in the same way as he administers a kingdom, being ignorant of the conditions which obtain in an army. This causes restlessness in the soldier's minds.

■ By employing the officers of his army without discrimination, through ignorance of the military principle of adaptation to circumstances. This shakes the confidence of the soldiers.

In the business world, a leader should know the strengths and weaknesses of their workforce. They must also ensure that their management – or officers – are of the right calibre and able to direct staff and seize opportunities for success as and when required.

As a business grows in size, so often does its workforce, requiring the owner to establish a management structure to enable it to continue to function with maximum efficiency. There are distinct challenges and opportunities faced by SMEs (small to medium-sized enterprises), though, in comparison to larger companies.

THE NEED FOR STRUCTURE

While a growing SME may want to retain the freethinking spirt of its early days, establishing some kind of management structure to cope with a burgeoning business can be unavoidable.

Having worked for large companies such as Coca-Cola and BT, Jeremy was determined not to recreate something with lots of layers and a big percentage of non revenue-generating workers. He initially tried to create a workforce of only client-facing staff. They were essentially one-man bands, talking to clients, writing proposals and then needing to deliver them and sort out all the paperwork.

'It was time inefficient, and whilst they may have had client in their title, only 25 per cent of their time was spent in that direction.'

So he brought in project managers to take the delivery side of the business off the hands of the client teams, then he brought in a web developer to run the digital aspects of the business and, before he knew it, his business had 25 staff.

At that point, he realized that he needed someone to manage the staff and the office, so he brought in his first HR manager and the dreaded layers he had not wanted to install soon started to appear. They now had job titles such as 'project executive', 'project coordinator', 'project manager', 'head of operations', and 'managing director' – all answering to Jeremy himself.

'It is annoying, it is a long chain but it does work – and crucially it provides the sort of growth opportunities that a flat structure does not really have.'

THE RIGHT PEOPLE

Sometimes, then, it becomes necessary not only to recruit, but to build a structure in your growing business. This, though, can present issues.

Stephanie identifies a particular problem when it comes to smaller, growing businesses: promotion is often the reward for someone who has excelled at one particular role. This might not always create a well-rounded manager, though, and may result in the wrong person being promoted – a move that is not only bad for the growing company but bad for the individuals themselves too.

Stephanie says: 'What's challenging with most small businesses is that they end up promoting someone who was great at one aspect of a job to be the manager, without checking to see whether that person has the character traits of a manager.

'When you ask the employee they will always say that they can do the manager job, but until they are in the midst of it, they may not realize how much they will hate it.

'For example, I worked with a client who had a really fantastic employee in one department, who was great at his job and did a great job training the new employees.

'When the department manager moved on, they promoted that employee to manager and he did great – for about six months.

'Then he started avoiding some of the managerial stuff that he didn't like, and things went downhill fast. The leadership tried to motivate him using calls to action and promises that didn't feed what drove that employee personally and it created frustration all around.'

RECRUITING MANAGERS

Like officers in an army, managers play a crucial role. An army without coordination is simply a group of people, all with different ideas and ways of approaching any given situation. An organization which is well managed, be it a military formation or a business, will be coordinated, everyone will know their place and purpose, and the group will be able to respond to changing situations at speed.

So when hiring managers, it is essential to have a robust and reliable process for their recruitment.

Stephanie says: 'I think it's important to use personality assessments as well as a thorough analysis process of why someone has succeeded in their current job, and what skillsets are necessary to become a manager or senior staff.'

Implementing testing as well as a highly structured interview process was something Jeremy had done at his own firm to enable him to find the right people. He says: 'No more of these casual hiring of a mate's third cousin. We interview over the phone, we then interview in person in a structured manner including a couple of tests for maths, verbal reasoning, logic and a legal technical one depending on the role, and finally we do a psychometric evaluation.

'None of the tests spell doom – attitude and skills are still vital – but they have been seen to be arbiters of success or failure in post.'

CUT YOUR LOSSES EARLY

Having the wrong people in senior positions can make or break an organization, so sometimes it is important to listen to your instincts as their leader and make tough decisions.

Cutting your losses early with a new member of the team is therefore very important, and Jeremy adds that if you think it's not working out with someone in the early days, then it probably never will.

'Too often I have delayed a decision, given them more time, but it rarely works out and we have wasted time and risked them infecting others.'

Another principal component of success when it comes to building a management team is having people the leader can trust. People who are pulling in the same direction and share the same vision and goals.

'I know they say to recruit "people who are brighter than you", but have they ever actually done? It is challenging – for both sides.

'What I have been able to achieve is solid, reliable people that I can trust – trust to do a job, but also trust to challenge me if they think a decision or a direction is not right.

'They are fully invested in the company and its ideals. We call it "purple blood" to match our corporate colour.

'My two right-hand people have both been with me for over nine years, one rising from account manager to deputy MD.'

REMEMBER EVERY ROLE IS DIFFERENT

When first building a management structure, it is important to remember that each department will demand a different set of very specific skills.

Stephanie says: 'Every culture and department is going to need different skillsets in their management. For example, a sales department manager might need the "golden tongue" and [a] high

people-engaging personality, whereas an admin/office manager might need to be more focused on SOPs [standard operating procedures] and following procedures.'

Apart from particular personality traits that may be useful for different departments, though, there are some common threads that your managers should have.

'In general, you need someone who thrives on a challenge, who has an extensive understanding of human psychology and knows not just how, but also why we do what we do.

'You need someone who understands the amount of energy necessary to stand up and motivate their team daily.'

CONCLUSIONS

Sun Tzu talked about the importance of swift success and not letting campaigns drag on needlessly. He also spoke of the importance of foraging for supplies where possible and also of having an organized force led by capable officers.

From a business perspective we can learn the following:

■ Beware the race to the bottom.

■ Understand the dangers of devaluing a market by lowering your prices too much.

■ Appoint the right people as managers.

■ Make sure your top people are there for the right reasons and will bring the right skills and knowledge to bear.

■ Cut your losses early.

■ If you make a wrong staffing decision, change course ASAP.

Attack by Stratagem

(Sun Tzu's Original Text)

1. Sun Tzu said: In the practical art of war, the best thing of all is to take the enemy's country whole and intact; to shatter and destroy it is not so good. So, too, it is better to recapture an army entire than to destroy it, to capture a regiment, a detachment or a company entire than to destroy them.

2. Hence to fight and conquer in all your battles is not supreme excellence; supreme excellence consists in breaking the enemy's resistance without fighting.

3. Thus the highest form of generalship is to balk the enemy's plans; the next best is to prevent the junction of the enemy's forces; the next in order is to attack the enemy's army in the field; and the worst policy of all is to besiege walled cities.

4. The rule is, not to besiege walled cities if it can possibly be avoided. The preparation of mantlets, movable shelters, and various implements of war, will take up three whole months; and the piling up of mounds against the walls will take three months more.

5.   The general, unable to control his irritation, will launch his men to the assault like swarming ants, with the result that one-third of his men are slain, while the town still remains untaken. Such are the disastrous effects of a siege.

6.   Therefore the skilful leader subdues the enemy's troops without any fighting; he captures their cities without laying siege to them; he overthrows their kingdom without lengthy operations in the field.

7.   With his forces intact he will dispute the mastery of the Empire, and thus, without losing a man, his triumph will be complete. This is the method of attacking by stratagem.

8. It is the rule in war, if our forces are ten to the enemy's one, to surround him; if five to one, to attack him; if twice as numerous, to divide our army into two.

9. If equally matched, we can offer battle; if slightly inferior in numbers, we can avoid the enemy; if quite unequal in every way, we can flee from him.

10. Hence, though an obstinate fight may be made by a small force, in the end it must be captured by the larger force.

11. Now the general is the bulwark of the State; if the bulwark is complete at all points, the State will be strong; if the bulwark is defective, the State will be weak.

12. There are three ways in which a ruler can bring misfortune upon his army:—

13. (1) By commanding the army to advance or to retreat, being ignorant of the fact that it cannot obey. This is called hobbling the army.

14. (2) By attempting to govern an army in the same way as he administers a kingdom, being ignorant of the conditions which obtain in an army. This causes restlessness in the soldier's minds.

15. (3) By employing the officers of his army without discrimination, through ignorance of the military principle of adaptation to circumstances. This shakes the confidence of the soldiers.

16. But when the army is restless and distrustful, trouble is sure to come from the other feudal princes. This is simply bringing anarchy into the army, and flinging victory away.

17. Thus we may know that there are five essentials for victory:
(1) He will win who knows when to fight and when not to fight.
(2) He will win who knows how to handle both superior and inferior forces.
(3) He will win whose army is animated by the same spirit throughout all its ranks.
(4) He will win who, prepared himself, waits to take the enemy unprepared.
(5) He will win who has military capacity and is not interfered with by the sovereign.

18. Hence the saying: If you know the enemy and know yourself, you need not fear the result of a hundred battles. If you know yourself but not the enemy, for every victory gained you will also suffer a defeat. If you know neither the enemy nor yourself, you will succumb in every battle.

CHAPTER 4

TACTICAL DISPOSITIONS

Tactics go hand in hand with strategy. While strategy is based around the achievement of longer-term goals, tactics are the day-to-day actions that bring those strategic goals closer.
In this chapter, Sun Tzu introduces us to two principal concepts crucial to success: securing your position from defeat; spotting opportunities for attack.
His first teaching was all about giving yourself a sure footing and establishing a secure position before attempting any forward moves. Essentially, ensuring you were safe from defeat first and foremost, before attempting to strike.

The good fighters of old first put themselves beyond the possibility of defeat, and then waited for an opportunity of defeating the enemy. To secure ourselves against defeat lies in our own hands, but the opportunity of defeating the enemy is provided by the enemy himself.

CONSOLIDATING YOUR POSITION

It can be easy to succumb to the excitement that building a business elicits. It is, after all, this passion that can be the difference between success and failure. But it is equally important not to pursue goals that will leave your business on a less than sure footing.

While new markets may be there for the taking or opportunities may seem ripe for the plucking, endeavours that require capital and manpower must not be pursued at the expense of the sure ground your current venture occupies.

While establishing your business and pondering new routes of expansion, be mindful of what you already have.

But before you think about going on to new victories, first secure yourself from defeat.

There are tried and trusted methods of securing a business against the buffering of waves and headwinds which may come its way.

BECOME FINANCIALLY RESILIENT

Finance is the lifeblood of any organization, and ensuring you are not paying out more than you have to is an important way of securing yourself against the threat of financial defeat.

Methods for this include:
■ profit and cash flow management;
■ reducing core outgoings;
■ taking on more roles yourself;
■ reducing property costs.

KEEPING AN EYE ON PROFIT AND CASH FLOW

Stephanie Scheller advises robust management of cashflow and profit when it comes to helping build financial resilience. This is especially useful during times of crises or when the company is struggling financially.

Managing cashflow entails:
■ pricing yourself for profit;
■ negotiating longer payment terms with your vendors.

Stephanie says: 'If you can get them (vendors) to give you 30, 60 or 90 days to pay an invoice, you can hold on to your cash longer and it gives you longer to get paid on the other side as well.

'The key is to ensure you are monitoring and managing the money you've received that is earmarked to pay them off and don't find yourself staring down a massive bill with no cash to pay it because you spent it elsewhere.'

Negotiating shorter payment terms with clients

'If you can arrange for your clients to pay upon receipt (or, better yet, at time of ordering!), you limit the amount of time you are out of pocket for paying cost of goods sold.

'Additionally, you might eliminate an entire department from your company and save on payroll as well as defaulted payments from vendors in the accounts receivable department.'

Use credit wisely

'Whether this is a loan, a line of credit or a credit card, don't use your credit to cover business maintenance bills like payroll.

'Credit should be used to cover bills you have cash on hand to pay if you want to build up rewards, or to take advantage of growth opportunities.'

PROFIT MANAGEMENT

If a company is to stay in business, let alone grow, it will need sooner or later to turn a profit. We've talked already about the danger of lowering prices too much and damaging a market, but beyond that, ensuring that you generate enough money will keep your company secure from financial peril, enabling you to grasp opportunities that come your way.

Stephanie says, 'You've got to price yourself profitably from the get-go! I highly recommend digging into the Mike Michalowicz's Profit First concept; but in short, whatever price point you put yourself at should provide room for 10 per cent to profits, 15 per cent for taxes, 10 per cent to marketing or commissions.

'And there should be room left in the remaining 65 per cent to cover the cost of goods sold as well as room to cover overheads, payroll, etc!

'Set the price you need and then find a way to be worth the price in your market.'

MAINTAIN YOUR MARGINS

Costs go up all the time – that is one harsh reality for any business – so in order to stay in profit it is essential to constantly monitor and review how much you are making and where improvements can be made.

'Build your brand, or review pricing regularly and protect those margins. There are a million things looking to eat their way into your profits (software subscriptions you forgot you signed up for, unexpected fees),' says Stephanie.

STOP THINKING LIKE AN EMPLOYEE

Many self-employed entrepreneurs may have previously worked for someone else and when it comes to getting paid, some may still not appreciate the difference between the two.

Stephanie said: 'Understand the difference between a profit margin and a pay cheque.

'You as the business owner deserve to receive profit distributions in exchange for the risk you've taken to start the business and the capital you've invested in the business.

'You deserve more than just a job and the opportunity to not have a boss. But too many business owners only profit a pay cheque or profit distributions for themselves.

'If you are working in your business, you need to be receiving a pay cheque for the work you're doing.

'If you're the owner of the business, you should also receive a regular profit distribution that is a bonus on top of the pay cheque you get monthly.'

REDUCING YOUR OUTGOINGS

They say the simple solutions are often the best, but it goes without saying that trimming fat from your outgoings is something every entrepreneur should do regularly. Every penny and cent is precious, and each adds up to potentially massive savings over the course of the year, which can help ensure greater resilience.

Cutting outgoings could mean:
- reducing staff numbers where roles are no longer crucial to maintaining business effectiveness;
- no longer subscribing to software you do not need, or finding a freeware alternative;
- reviewing costs for things like utilities, broadband, insurance, IT or accountancy services.

One effective idea is creating a cash flow plan for the next 12 months and also working out how much income your businesses needs to keep it afloat for the next six months. For many businesses this will take you to the end of the tax year, which is a good time to reassess.

CUTTING SUBSCRIPTIONS

Many of today's businesses are hugely reliant on digital services and software, and many of them can incur expensive initial fees and recurring subscriptions. You should perform regular audits of what software you have and what you actually need. You may be surprised at how bloated your IT has become – and this will free up not only cash but also physical space on your network.

BECOME AN ALL-ROUNDER

As businesses grow, so does confidence, and many entrepreneurs who start off as a one-person operation soon begin to bring aboard contractors or to outsource aspects of what they do, such as marketing strategy or social media.

But in order to keep outgoings to a minimum, an entrepreneur should consider what they can do with their existing resources first, either by utilizing the existing skillsets already present in their team, or simply taking on those roles themselves.

Accessing training providers to learn new skills is also something that could help enable you to take on more roles and cut costs. Organizations such as Future Learn and Google Digital Garage, for instance, offer access to free training on subjects such as social media and marketing.

FLEXIBLE OFFICE SPACE

Alongside staffing, property is often the biggest expense for any business, and this is something that has come very much to the fore during the COVID-19 pandemic. The virus's impact on business and its aftermath have probably changed how we will work forever, with more people likely to work from home for at least part of their week.

Some business leaders, though, have not given up on the office completely, with high-profile figures such as Goldman Sachs CEO David Solomon and Jes Staley, Chief Executive of Barclays Bank, advocating a return to office working.

It is most likely that businesses will find some degree of compromise between home and office working, with a 'hybrid model' becoming the new normal for many companies.

This model involves staff working from home when appropriate, but then coming into a physical office space for things such as team catch-ups and client meetings.

But even before the pandemic hit, global business was warming to the idea of a flexible office model as a way to cut back on property costs as well as provide a better work and life balance for employees.

Figures compiled by Instant Offices[1] found that the flexible office market had grown by 50 per cent during the last five years.

---

1   https://www.instantoffices.com/blog/featured/flex-workspace-trends-2019-beyond/

These types of deals allow companies to avoid making long-term financial commitments and instead hire the exact amount of desk space they need, complete with costs thrown in such as internet and phones, reception services and access to meeting rooms.

Crucially, they are often on rolling contracts, too, meaning companies can keep their outgoings under constant review.

The pandemic has only sped up this move away from a traditional office, meaning there are clear opportunities now to save money by only leasing property as and when you need it, for the exact amount of staff you require. The cost-saving of such a model is potentially huge.

STAYING AHEAD OF THE CURVE

The second important principle for Sun Tzu in this chapter was that once secure from the possibility of defeat, the would-be victor had to identify and seize opportunities to strike.

> **To see victory only when it is within the ken of the common herd is not the acme of excellence.**

This is arguably the most important aspect of any entrepreneur and the aspect which sets them apart from other people.

There is no definitive list of types of entrepreneur, but one thing the successful ones all share is the ability to spot what is 'missing'.

Entrepreneurs look at the world around them and identify where the gaps are, whether it is a product or a service, and then they try to identify how they can provide it.

This means the entrepreneur must at first see the opportunities, but just as crucially, they should be ready and able to take the leap when those opportunities arise.

BE READY FOR THAT BIG WAVE

Australia may be known for its awesome surfing, but opportunity can also come in waves too.

Serial entrepreneur Joe Wehbe is CEO of Sydney Listings, a real estate company specializing in property management, as well as education start-up Doohat Labs.

He embraces the spirit of both of Sun Tzu's teachings in this chapter. Not only does he live a lifestyle that maintains cash liquidity for when he needs it, he also maintains a constant watch for potential new opportunities.

'If we were to think of problem-solving as surfing, then the market and opportunities are the waves that come along, and the bigger the wave, the better the chance of doing what we need to do. But we must be prepared, we must be in the water.'

MINIMUM VIABLE LIFESTYLE

In order to protect his finances while waiting for opportunities, Joe says he personally adopts the concept of 'minimum viable lifestyle'.

'The concept revolves around two questions.

'The first is: What's the least my life can be? The second is: What's the least income I need, that life is comfortable and happy, that my survival needs are met?

'Many people will be aware of the "ramen diet" from Silicon Valley circles, as the ultimate symbol of keeping expenses low, so that an entrepreneur can scrape by.

'As a very young entrepreneur, this is something which helps keep perspective and maximizes my liquidity so that when the right wave comes along, I recognize that it fits my criteria.'

KEEPING AN EYE ON THE BIG PICTURE

For Carla Williams Johnson, working in a smaller market such as the Caribbean can prove a challenge, and she has seen many fellow entrepreneurs fail.

Keeping a constant watch on what is happening around you, on the market and how rivals succeed or flounder is absolutely crucial to being able to spot opportunities when they arise.

'I know a few people who did attempt it but didn't quite make it,' says Carla.

'I believe it was because they got caught up in the idea of owning their own business and how simple things would be when they got all these new clients, but then reality set in and I think they realized how hard it was to consistently put themselves out there to build a brand. It didn't seem as easy and "fun" anymore.'

Just as Sun Tzu says that knowledge of yourself and your opponent adds up to powerful a formula for success, so the same is true, according to Carla, when trying to identify new opportunities.

The techniques she advises are:
■ researching the market to ensure your products or services are needed, wanted and priced competitively;
■ knowing who your target audience is and forming a deep relationship with them, both online and offline;
■ understanding what makes you unique and why people should buy from you over anyone else.

PASSION IS KEY

For most entrepreneurs, though, it is not as simple as spotting an opportunity.

While that is an important part of what can make a new venture a success, most successful entrepreneurs have first hit upon an idea by encountering a problem that they have been passionate about trying to fix.

Without a genuine desire to make something a success which transcends simple financial gain, it can be difficult to persevere through the difficult days, especially early on, when income can be modest or even non-existent.

Having that belief and that desire is something that can spur an entrepreneur on and, in many cases, it is that fire which is the difference between those that do not make it, and those that do.

TACTICAL DISPOSITIONS

On a personal level, Saasha Celestial-One feels there are two approaches to entrepreneurship:

■ Find a problem you are so passionate about solving that you are literally compelled to make it your life's mission to do so – validate the opportunity afterwards.

■ Like an investor, become an expert in pattern recognition. An aspiring entrepreneur without an opportunity can immerse themselves in podcasts, start-up blogs, follow investors/entrepreneurs on Twitter and engage in the conversation, etc. Then, perhaps an opportunity will present itself and you will be alert enough to spot it early.

This need for passion and belief in what you are doing is a principle with which Carla Williams Johnson absolutely agrees.

'There are days I feel like crying my eyes out because I'm doing so much and I feel like I've made so little progress; other times I feel like I'm just so exhausted from overworking, but I know I have to keep going.

'I know there are people out there who need me in their lives because they just can't figure things out themselves. They need an expert who is honest and reliable who'll tell them exactly what they need to build their business.'

She adds that one of the things which keeps her going is asking herself why she set off on this path in the first place and remembering what spurred her to get through those tough times.

'One of the things that absolutely keeps me going is getting back to why. From early on, I was tired of seeing business owners being taken advantage of by greedy consultants who were using their lack of knowledge against them in order to sell them packages or services that did nothing for their business.

'These consultants would just consistently line their pockets and not give any real value, and I was so appalled that someone whose main goal should be to help would just take people's hard-earned money like that.

65

'For me, one of my highest values is honesty. That's why I get so upset and it's the reason I cannot give up.

'I've actually been accused of over-delivering because I am so committed to ensuring that every client that I work with understands what strategies and tactics are right for them, so that they can make the impact and the income they deserve.'

Carla's advice is to ask:
- What makes you passionate?
- What keeps you going?
- What are the issues that keep the people you are trying to serve up at night?
- What problems can you solve and what relief can you bring to them?

She adds: 'These are the important questions to ask yourself before you jump into the business world. There are opportunities to serve everywhere, you just have to take notice and, once identified, start putting your plan of action into place.'

CONCLUSIONS

Sun Tzu spoke of two main areas here. The importance of securing yourself from defeat first and foremost, and then striking when you can.

From a business perspective we can learn the following:

■ Stay financially sound.

■ Be careful with money and ensure your company remains on a firm financial footing. Even if you are not expanding or pursuing new opportunities, you will hold on to what you already have.

■ Learn to spot opportunities.

■ Monitor the market in detail. Ensure you have a plan of action, so that when an opportunity arises, you are ready to take full advantage.

Tactical Dispositions

(Sun Tzu's Original Text)

1. Sun Tzu said: The good fighters of old first put themselves beyond the possibility of defeat, and then waited for an opportunity of defeating the enemy.

2. To secure ourselves against defeat lies in our own hands, but the opportunity of defeating the enemy is provided by the enemy himself.

3. Thus the good fighter is able to secure himself against defeat, but cannot make certain of defeating the enemy.

4. Hence the saying: One may know how to conquer without being able to do it.

5. Security against defeat implies defensive tactics; ability to defeat the enemy means taking the offensive.

6. Standing on the defensive indicates insufficient strength; attacking, a superabundance of strength.

7. The general who is skilled in defence hides in the most secret recesses of the earth; he who is skilled in attack flashes forth from the topmost heights of heaven. Thus on the one hand we have the ability to protect ourselves; on the other, a victory that is complete.

8. To see victory only when it is within the ken of the common herd is not the acme of excellence.

9. Neither is it the acme of excellence if you fight and conquer and the whole Empire says: 'Well done!'

10. To lift an autumn leaf is no sign of great strength; to see the sun and moon is no sign of sharp sight; to hear the noise of thunder is no sign of a quick ear.

11. What the ancients called a clever fighter is one who not only wins, but excels in winning with ease.

12. Hence his victories bring him neither reputation for wisdom nor credit for courage.

13. He wins his battles by making no mistakes. Making no mistakes is what establishes the certainty of victory, for it means conquering an enemy that is already defeated.

14. Hence the skilful fighter puts himself into a position which makes defeat impossible, and does not miss the moment for defeating the enemy.

15. Thus it is that in war the victorious strategist only seeks battle after the victory has been won, whereas he who is destined to defeat first fights and afterwards looks for victory.

16. The consummate leader cultivates the Moral Law, and strictly adheres to method and discipline; thus it is in his power to control success.

17. In respect of military method, we have, firstly, Measurement; secondly, Estimation of quantity; thirdly, Calculation; fourthly, Balancing of chances; fifthly, Victory.

18. Measurement owes its existence to Earth; Estimation of quantity to Measurement; Calculation to Estimation of quantity; Balancing of chances to Calculation; and Victory to Balancing of chances.

19. A victorious army opposed to a routed one, is as a pound's weight placed in the scale against a single grain.

20. The onrush of a conquering force is like the bursting of pent-up waters into a chasm a thousand fathoms deep.

CHAPTER 5

ENERGY

Sun Tzu talked of energy as the combination of direct and indirect methods of advancement, the flow and movements of an army in the face of an opponent's attacks or resistance, and the methods by which that army is governed and controlled.

So what does this actually mean? In essence, energy is what drives the army in its efforts towards victory, how it responds to obstacles, and how both of these things are handled by the control and governance of a leader and his commanders.

BIG VS SMALL

In Sun Tzu's view, the size of an army is unimportant in terms of how it is controlled and functions. In a modern business context, he would say that fundamentally, directing a business's operations is no different for an SME than it is for a multinational corporate powerhouse.

The control of a large force is of the same principle as the control of a few men. It is merely a question of dividing up their numbers.

More compact organizations can indeed be more flexible and nimble, able to respond quickly to challenges and varying market conditions, while larger companies may find that changing direction is like turning around an oil tanker.

SCALING DOWN WHAT ALREADY WORKS

Many entrepreneurs will have worked in larger corporations before they struck out on their own. In a lot of cases, the frustrations they encountered there may have played a part in inspiring their decision to start their own business in the first place.

While storming out that door and charting a course for solo success, it is important not to throw the baby out with the bathwater and instead to try to retain the best aspects of what makes a big company successful, while condensing it into something more manageable.

'There are a lot of lessons to be learned from larger organizations, and I've realized it is all about taking what has worked for them and scaling it down to suit your brand and build from there,' says Carla Williams Johnson.

EMBRACE YOUR PLACE IN THE MARKET

Carla feels that big companies often have a much more established sense of place and purpose in comparison with smaller ones, seeking instead to work within a market rather than measure their success by how they eclipse competitors. Seeing rivals as an opportunity, rather than simply a threat, is something some SMEs can learn from.

'Big businesses understand that everyone has their place, and they don't see their competition as their enemy but as an entity they can learn from or even collaborate with. These are the things small businesses need to adopt in order to achieve success.'

FEAR OF FAILURE

Like Carla, Jeremy Stern also worked in multinational corporations before flying solo. He says that one of the big advantages smaller organizations have over larger ones is the ability to take more risks.

'Big companies tend to be weighed down by bureaucracy and fear of failure.

'No one wants to risk being involved in something that does not work, so they choose mediocrity.

'And too often the big companies define themselves by the business that they are in, not [by the] businesses of the future or where they could be.

'Did sat navs come out of one of the big electronic giants? No.

'Did fitness bands come from a watch company or multinational tech company? No

'Did Wi-Fi doorbells come from an established player? No.

'They all came from outsiders, mavericks with a new idea and a passion to succeed.'

STRIKING A BALANCE

The flip side of this coin, according to Jeremy, is that failure rarely constitutes a major financial disaster for a big company, but could do so for a small company, so SMEs need to be careful.

The solution at PromoVeritas has been to try and strike a balance by making new services relatable to their core strategy, so that customers understand what value they bring straight from the off.

'At PromoVeritas we have tried and experimented with a number of new services, but we have always sought to stay true to our core – so [that means] linked services not separate, new "left-field" services.

'In this way, they will appeal to our existing client and, crucially, management will not get completely distracted by the "shiny new idea" and forget about the bit that really makes the money.'

COMBINING METHODS

As mentioned earlier, Sun Tzu was no conventional military chief. He was a strategist who embraced all methods in pursuit of victory and spoke of the importance of 'direct and indirect' methods.

In battle, there are not more than two methods of attack – the direct and the indirect; yet these two in combination give rise to an endless series of manoeuvres.

Direct methods were traditional military tactics, be they the use of archers and chariots engaging in combat, or siege tactics.

Indirect methods of attack could be more subtle, such as espionage or what would one day be known as propaganda. Through combining all or some of these methods, there was a panoply of possible attack methods at a commander's disposal.

In the context of finding success in the business world, it is equally important to deploy a wide range of tactics aimed at achieving success.

DIRECT AND INDIRECT

In the business world we most often see the concept of direct and indirect applied to sales.

The concept of direct sales is relatively straightforward and involves staff actively taking actions to engage a client. This can involve techniques such as:

- cold calling;
- direct emails;
- targeted social media ads;
- paid advertising;
- mailshots.

Indirect methods can involve a range of activities designed to create a positive brand image and ensure that when a potential customer is in need of a product or service, they are not only aware of your company's existence but also have a positive opinion of it.

Methods can include:
- being active on social media;
- having a website with good-quality SEO;
- investing in your brand image;
- positive online reviews;
- PR campaigns;
- word of mouth.

Indirect methods remain far less understood, and to this day, even concepts such as SEO and brand image can be misunderstood by some modern businesses, both big and small.

HELPING THEM FIND YOU

SEO – or search engine optimization – means the techniques used to ensure a website ranks higher on Google. The methods have changed massively over the last decade, and in some cases, companies have not kept pace with these developments.

Google works by using computer programmes called web crawlers to search websites for search terms typed by users into Google's search bar.

Way back when, some companies tried to 'game' Google by engaging in practices such as keyword stuffing, with blocks of repetitive text arranged haphazardly on the page. This is something we have all probably read from time to time.

In practice this could mean that if someone was searching for a 'red car', the web copy could read as follows: 'If you're looking for a red car, this is the best place to find a red car, red cars are great, everyone loves a red car.'

In the past, Google would have scanned the phrase 'red car' and elevated the website in its rankings, but when human eyes read the text they would have been disappointed, to say the least.

As time went by, Google has released multiple updates to its algorithm – the exact workings of which are still a closely guarded secret – which means that these short cuts no longer work. In fact, a website with poor content may be penalized and drop down the rankings.

Now, in order to rank well on Google, websites need quality content that is original, readable and shareable. A company that wishes to enhance the searchability of their website should consider investing time in their SEO. Not only will it be a more pleasant experience for visitors, it will also help push the site up those rankings too.

PR CAMPAIGNS

Public relations may seem like the domain of the multinational, but Carla says there is an abundance of opportunities out there for SMEs if they take the right approach.

Handled correctly, it can not only be done for little or even no cost, but also – she argues – add more authenticity to the direct sales method of 'paid for' ads.

'Getting featured in traditional media has helped many of my clients increase their online engagement by as much as 80 per cent when the links are shared on their social media pages, while others have experienced an increase in opt-ins and have even gotten requests to be paid to share their knowledge.

'Many have noted that the day they're featured they experience a marginal increase in sales of their programs, packages and masterminds.'

She says there are many different ways to get featured, including:
- guest posts/blogs;
- round-ups;
- podcast interviews;
- magazine and press features;
- television interviews;
- radio interviews;
- speaker/panel discussions.

She adds: 'So whether you'd prefer to write, speak, contribute to part of a feature or [have] an entire article all about you, there is a media house out there that will love to hear from you, and many of them would gladly feature you at no cost because they're always looking for content that inspires, motivates and educates their audience.

'It's really something all business owners should consider because social media is important but lacks credibility because it's overflowing with 'so-called' experts. Paid ads are great but [are] biased and lack authenticity, but PR is truly one of the most powerful tools you can use and it's free!'

HERO BRANDS AND AUTHENTICITY

As social media has evolved, it has become less about sharing random tweets or Facebook updates designed to gain likes and shares from customers and potential customers, but about an overall strategy designed to establish a brand.

Newer players, such as Instagram and TikTok, mean that multiple channels are now available, from video to sound and images. These let business owners establish a brand that has value and which inspires loyalty and even love.

In essence, modern businesses use social media to create fans as well as customers, people who will not just buy your product but will actively root for your success. Having a brand 'story' is essential to creating this.

'At the end of the day, your brand has to stand for something and it's more than just a fancy logo or your brand's colours, but how you want people to feel and that emotional connection,' says Carla.

'It's about your brand values and how you want to be represented. It's allowing that authenticity [to] shine through and being unapologetic about it.

'So, showcasing the things that are real to you and, of course, the clients you're wanting to serve is truly the best way to show up. Sometimes it may not always be pretty, but I guarantee that realness would resonate and be so relatable that people would love you even more.'

BUILDING A POSITIVE IMAGE

Turning people into fans as well as customers is easier said than done. More and more companies of all sizes are realizing the importance of aligning themselves with issues that matter to people, whether it is environmentalism or equality.

CHAPTER 5

'Promoting a positive image of your business really comes down to understanding what your core values are and sticking to them,' says Stephanie Scheller.

'When you've got a potential marketing opportunity that isn't sitting well with your gut where your advertiser is trying to tell you to tear someone else down, or make a claim that isn't fully honest, you have to stand up for yourself and stick to what's true and what you want to reflect you.'

Of course, one of the downsides of social media is that it can be a polarizing place given to disagreements and negativity. With that in mind, Stephanie strongly cautions that you keep messages confined to specific areas.

'I encourage businesses to stay out of three things: smut, politics and religion. There's no way to come out of that smelling clean and maintaining a positive image.'

RELEASING THE BOW

Sun Tzu says that energy may be likened to the bending of a crossbow and decision is like the releasing of a trigger. Therefore, as well as having energy in the organization and the ability for it to be mobilized into action, the leader must be decisive and be ready to fire that arrow when the time comes.

The quality of decision is like the well-timed swoop of a falcon which enables it to strike and destroy its victim.

BEING DECISIVE

Decision-making is crucial in any entrepreneur. The ability to release that arrow at the right time, and in the right circumstances, can be the difference between those who succeed and those who do not.

'Decisiveness is critical, and I would say it is one of the areas I've improved on most in my entrepreneurial adventures so far. And I've learned it the hard way,' says Joe Wehbe.

ENERGY

The Sydney-based entrepreneur started his career with a non-profit in Nepal before changing his focus to real estate. During this time, he said he experienced long periods of indecision, particularly over bigger issues such as what type of service to focus on or specialise in.

> **Indecision is a sure sign that one lacks clarity, and clarity is the most important of the assets, it's really the beginning of the journey. How can you do anything if you aren't clear on what you're doing or why? – Joe Wehbe**

INFORMED DECISIONS

Recognizing the need to be more decisive is one thing, but it's easier said than done. Self-doubt and 'what if' are central components of the human condition, but there are ways of ensuring you have the tools you need at your disposal to inform those decisions.

This is something Saasha Celestial-One and her business partner have developed to help them with their own business.

'Tessa and I are extremely fast decision-makers.

'We've developed a process that we've perfected over the years. It helps that we're both trained management consultants, and keen advocates of the principles of the Lean Startup.'

Their system involves the following actions:
- Set up the problem you are trying to solve or the decision you are trying to make properly – what is the context, what is the decision, why is it important, what are all of the options?
- Form one or more hypotheses, including the 'why' something will work and the 'what' will happen if it does.
- Ascertain the minimum amount of critical information required to prove or disprove the hypotheses, and start collecting data.
- Meanwhile, interview 5–10 experts who have been there, done that and can

79

help you get up to speed quickly. (Patterns will also emerge.) Write down all of your notes verbatim, as you will review them later

■ Validate or invalidate your hypothesis – either is fine.

Saasha says: 'We both often joke that becoming mothers really improved our decision-making speed and skills, but it's true – when under pressure, you learn to hone in on the most critical information to quickly inform your decisions.

For example, we recently launched a whole new section in the app, called MADE, where users can sell delicious homemade food and sustainable handmade crafts to each other. 'From ideation to launch +7,500 pre-registered Makers, was four months.

'It was critical that we moved quickly so as to not miss October to December – peak sales season for Christmas gifts.

'There's definitely an element of "building the airplane as you fly", but also being hyper-efficient and not being afraid to make small mistakes in order to maintain momentum.'

MAKE DECISIONS ALIGNED TO YOUR VALUES
Carla once again advocates looking deeper at your motivation for decisions and says it is important to trust your own instincts: 'I've learned that for every decision I make, it must be in alignment with my values.

'I've learned to trust my intuition and have adapted a more purpose-driven approach and I've found that working in this way has allowed me to attract the best customers, the most lucrative business deals and has really allowed me to show up and connect deeper with my audience.'

She adds: 'It's a work in progress, but the more aligned I feel, the easier it is to make decisions that are best for me and my business.'

DON'T DWELL TOO MUCH ON YOUR DECISIONS
It was the Roman scholar and statesman Marcus Tullius Cicero who said: 'More is lost by indecision than wrong decision.'

In that spirit, it is crucial that as well as being decisive, you do not let the fear of making the wrong choice hamper your progress.

Joe says he operates a decision-making framework he calls 'The thousand doors'.

'It's based on the metaphor that each of us is going through business and life through a series of rooms and "doors".

'We don't always know what lies on the other side of a door, but the longer we stay in one room trying to make a decision, the less momentum and learning we can enjoy.'

We are wired to seek certainty when we make a decision. The only problem with that is that real opportunity lies buried in uncertainty – Joe Wehbe.

KEEP TRYING DOORS

Wehbe says that one thing he has learned is not to fuss over making the perfect decision – and when you realize that if you have entered the wrong room, just choose a new door quickly.

'If we don't like the next room, just open another door sooner. Each door gives us the opportunity to learn more and more, to work on our judgement, and improve as we go.

'Learning comes from going through doors, not sitting rooted in one room. So the advice I give to myself is keep moving through doors, learning as you go.'

MOMENTUM IS CRUCIAL

Once energy is built and released at the appropriate time, Sun Tzu said it was crucial to keep that momentum going if the chances of victory were to be maximized.

Thus the energy developed by good fighting men is as the momentum of a round stone rolled down a

mountain thousands of feet in height. So much on the subject of energy.

So too, is it crucial to maintain momentum in business – particularly in the start-up phase. Saasha says the best way of doing this is via constant communication with all parties.

'It's incredibly important to maintain momentum and communicate this to all stakeholders – investors, press, employees, and customers!

'The way we do this is continuously celebrating and communicating wins and milestones. It could be as simple as a touching human story, about how your product or service has changed someone's life.

'Get their permission to share their quote and celebrate this achievement by sharing broadly.

'Or it could be a commercial or impact milestone – don't be shy to let everyone know. Drip-feeding good news to all stakeholders is a great way to keep the wind in your sails.'

CONCLUSION

Sun Tzu spoke of energy as that force which carries an army forward, of how smaller forces and larger ones can be controlled in a similar way, and of direct and indirect methods that could be employed to secure victory.

In a business context, this means:

■ Size doesn't always matter.

■ A smaller company can function just like a larger one, simply scaled down. It can also have advantages over bigger players.

■ There are indirect and direct routes to success.

■ Whether it is effective SEO or building a hero brand, there are ways to improve a company's chances of success which are not directly related to direct sales.

■ Being decisive is crucial.

■ Making decisions and maintaining the momentum of a successful business are both crucial factors in determining the success of a venture.

Energy

(Sun Tzu's Original Text)

1. Sun Tzu said: The control of a large force is the same principle as the control of a few men: it is merely a question of dividing up their numbers.

2. Fighting with a large army under your command is nowise different from fighting with a small one: it is merely a question of instituting signs and signals.

3. To ensure that your whole host may withstand the brunt of the enemy's attack and remain unshaken – this is effected by manoeuvres direct and indirect.

4. That the impact of your army may be like a grindstone dashed against an egg – this is effected by the science of weak points and strong.

5. In all fighting, the direct method may be used for joining battle, but indirect methods will be needed in order to secure victory.

6. Indirect tactics, efficiently applied, are inexhaustible as Heaven and Earth, unending as the flow of rivers and streams; like the sun and moon, they end but to begin anew; like the four seasons, they pass away to return once more.

7.   There are not more than five musical notes, yet the combinations of these five give rise to more melodies than can ever be heard.

8.   There are not more than five primary colours (blue, yellow, red, white and black), yet in combination they produce more hues than can ever be seen.

9.   There are not more than five cardinal tastes (sour, acrid, salt, sweet and bitter), yet combinations of them yield more flavours than can ever be tasted.

10.   In battle, there are not more than two methods of attack – the direct and the indirect; yet these two in combination give rise to an endless series of manoeuvres.

11.   The direct and the indirect lead on to each other in turn. It is like moving in a circle – you never come to an end. Who can exhaust the possibilities of their combination?

12.   The onset of troops is like the rush of a torrent which will even roll stones along in its course.

13.   The quality of decision is like the well-timed swoop of a falcon which enables it to strike and destroy its victim.

14.   Therefore the good fighter will be terrible in his onset, and prompt in his decision.

15.   Energy may be likened to the bending of a crossbow; decision, to the releasing of a trigger.

16. Amid the turmoil and tumult of battle, there may be seeming disorder and yet no real disorder at all; amid confusion and chaos, your array may be without head or tail, yet it will be proof against defeat.

17. Simulated disorder postulates perfect discipline, simulated fear postulates courage; simulated weakness postulates strength.

18. Hiding order beneath the cloak of disorder is simply a question of subdivision; concealing courage under a show of timidity presupposes a fund of latent energy; masking strength with weakness is to be effected by tactical dispositions.

19. Thus one who is skilful at keeping the enemy on the move maintains deceitful appearances, according to which the enemy will act. He sacrifices something, that the enemy may snatch at it.

20. By holding out baits, he keeps him on the march; then with a body of picked men he lies in wait for him.

21. The clever combatant looks to the effect of combined energy, and does not require too much from individuals. Hence his ability to pick out the right men and utilize combined energy.

22. When he utilizes combined energy, his fighting men become as it were like unto rolling logs or stones. For it is the nature of a log or stone to remain motionless on level ground, and to move when on a slope; if four-cornered, to come to a standstill, but if round-shaped, to go rolling down.

23. Thus the energy developed by good fighting men is as the momentum of a round stone rolled down a mountain thousands of feet in height. So much on the subject of energy.

CHAPTER 6

WEAK POINTS AND STRONG

In this chapter Sun Tzu focuses on a number of key themes, namely the need to be first and the advantages presented by imposing your will on the enemy.

As anyone who has ever been to an interview or important meeting will know, it is never a good idea to be late and flustered. Not only does this present a bad image, but it can also leave you unable to be at your very best at a crucial moment.

Sun Tzu believed that armies operated in the same way. The combat formations that reached the battlefield first would be able to establish themselves in good time. They could prepare themselves both mentally and physically for what was to come.

Conversely, a combatant who was last to the battlefield would be forced to join battle on the opponent's terms. There would not be time to prepare, or to size up the battlefield or the ground around it – an instant disadvantage.

Whoever is first in the field and awaits the coming of the enemy, will be fresh for the fight; whoever is second in the field and has to hasten to battle will arrive exhausted.

In a business context, establishing a presence in a market first allows an entrepreneur to set the tone for that market. If done successfully, they can become the 'go-to' business for that market. The term for this is 'first mover'.

FIRST MOVER ADVANTAGE

A first mover is a product or a service that achieves a competitive advantage quite simply by being first to market.

This presents it with a number of benefits, collectively known as 'first mover advantage':

- the ability to establish a product or service as the industry standard;
- tapping into customers first and establishing strong brand recognition and loyalty;
- having the time to establish links with suppliers and to position yourself strategically in the market;
- the potential to make the cost of switching from your product to a new competitor prohibitive.

There are potential disadvantages to be aware of too:

- new rivals can learn from your mistakes and improve on your offering;
- you may invest in creating brand awareness for a new product, only for a rival to take advantage.

A number of high-profile and successful companies have been first movers, including eBay, Nasdaq and Amazon.

BOOKS ONLINE

Amazon may be a global powerhouse in e-commerce today, but it started as a simple proposition – it sold books online.

In 1994, the company's founder Jeff Bezos – a former banker and hedge fund manager – incorporated Amazon.com.[1] After conducting his own research, he decided that books would be the most logical product to sell online.

---

1   https://www.britannica.com/topic/Amazoncom

Bezos initially named the company Cadabra but later changed it to Amazon after the river in South America, the largest in the world and arguably the longest. Not only did he get the benefit of that association, but the name begins with the letter A, the first letter of the alphabet.

By being an online bookseller with no bricks and mortar stores, the company was able to stay financially lean in comparison with its high street counterparts. It also became a first mover in this particular space of the market.

All future opponents in the space would have to rush to meet Amazon on its own terms. By this point, however, it had already established brand loyalty. It was the go-to company for buying books online, and it was able to establish its own terms, pricing and conventions by which all future rivals would be judged.

Such was its success that few if any online booksellers were able to come anywhere close to its market share.

In the context of Sun Tzu's teachings, being first to the battlefield and establishing its presence early enabled Amazon to achieve a decisive victory.

THE ART OF DISRUPTION

In this chapter, Sun Tzu also said it was crucial for a commander to impose themselves on their opponent – rather than let the opponent impose themselves.

> ## Therefore the clever combatant imposes his will on the enemy, but does not allow the enemy's will to be imposed on him.

Central to this concept in a business context is 'disruption'.

The words disruption and disruptor have passed into the business vernacular in recent years and are synonymous with radical breaks from convention and finding new and different ways of doing things.

Frequently this has enabled start-ups, particularly tech start-ups, to have a significant impact on traditional markets that often belie their smaller stature.

This term also relates to the notion of changing an existing market irrevocably. As Sun Tzu would say – imposing your will upon it, dictating the new terms and the new rules by which it is now governed.

In the world of finance, transportation and travel, disruption has been a key factor in recent years. Harnessing tech such as smartphones and apps, new players have been able to alter these long-established markets. Airbnb, for example, is a hotel chain that owns no property. Instead, they lease out people's homes and connect them with would-be guests who wish to stay there, all using an app or website.

Likewise, the financial technology industry, or 'fintech', has exploded over the last decade, enabling services such as digital currency and peer-to-peer lending. For the first time ever, traditional banks, many of which have been around for hundreds of years, are not only having to contend with new entrants to their market, they are actively having to adjust how they themselves do business in response to companies that are now shifting the boundaries of what is possible. The battle lines have been redrawn.

A HOTEL COMPANY WITH NO HOTELS?

It all started with a single email.

'Brian. I thought of a way to make a few bucks – turning our place into a designers' bed and breakfast.'

Those few words laid the foundation for one of the most disruptive companies in history, Airbnb.

It was back in 2007 that one of the company's co-founders, Joe Gebbia, found himself broke and on the lookout to make some extra money.

He noticed that all the hotels in San Francisco where he lived were booked up ahead of a design conference, so he emailed his roommate Brian Chesky about renting their place out as somewhere to stay. They set up three air mattresses (hence where 'air' comes in) and a website and managed to rent them out to three designers.

Along with their old roommate Nathan Blecharczyk, they then decided to try and turn it into a business. It was not plain sailing at first, with people finding it hard to get comfortable with the idea of letting strangers into their home.

The trio was also repeatedly rejected by investors who were not sold on the concept.

Fast forward to today and the company now has 5.6 million listings in more than 220 countries. But as Chesky has said in the past, 'Our "overnight" success took 1,000 days.'

Airbnb works by allowing people to register their homes online in the same way you would advertise a hotel. Potential guests view the listings and reviews and choose where they want to stay. The person leasing the property then receives money from the guest and Airbnb gets a commission.

The company has not been without its controversies, but it has completely disrupted the hotel market. Hotel companies have traditionally been able to charge a premium on the most sought-after tourist and business locations, such as New York and London, largely because there was high demand and only a finite number of hotels.

But because of this new business model, every spare room in those cities is now a potential place to stay. This has led to a loss of revenue for the hospitality industry, but it has also witnessed the sector adapt to a world where Airbnb is here to stay. This has helped keep costs lower for customers and also seen some hotel companies embrace the concept of 'being local' rather than simply one of a chain. The idea of being embedded in the local community is one of Airbnb's selling points and something the wider sector has tried to take onboard.

Some hotel companies have even started advertising their rooms on Airbnb's website.

So Airbnb had not just managed to shake up a traditional industry – one which has been around in some form or another, largely unchanged, for thousands of years – it has forced it to adapt.

As Sun Tzu said, Airbnb imposed their will upon their rivals.

BIG OR SMALL – DISRUPTION IS A MINDSET

Companies like Airbnb are global, but you don't have to rock the foundations of the world to be a disruptor. The impact you have is not measured in geographical terms, but more by how much you impact the status quo.

Stephanie Scheller's company is not only disruptive, but she has worked with disruptors extensively. She says that when it comes to shaking the foundations, the focus should be what works for you and your business goals.

'So often we have this idea that to be a disruptor we have to blow the whole world up.

'But your world is only as big or small as you want it to be. You can decide to focus on rewriting the expectations of your industry in your hometown only or take it out to a global level if you want.'

CHOOSE AN ASPECT TO DISRUPT

Disruption does not have to take the form of some sort of tech upheaval or app-led revolution. It can simply be a case of creating a new revenue stream that other people simply may not have tried before, or that they did not think was possible.

For example, when Stephanie's company started putting on events, she said many people told her that she needed to sell things at those events in order to make money. But she did not agree.

'The more I looked at the industry, though, I realized that what they were telling me was based on an industry expectation of an event being full of pitches and a waste of people's time.

'So of course no one wants to pay a substantial amount of money to attend an event that is a big sales pitch.

'So I listened to what they had to share, but I realized that if I build a brand of exceptional quality, I could charge enough to make money on the front end and if people knew that what to expect, they would pay it.

'It took a few years of losing money on events for people to realize that they could confidently pay the higher fee up front and they would enjoy the event more because of it because we weren't like other events in the growth industry.'

By gradually reshaping a potential customer's expectations of these types of events, she was able, over time, to convince people of their value. This in itself was a disruptive move: Stephanie had shifted the boundaries.

BE THE VOICE OF CHANGE

Making decisive business decisions that result in success will itself prove disruptive to a market as customer expectations are reshaped and potential rivals try to mimic your success. This is a passive form of disruption, but there are more active methods too – namely, being a cheerleader for change.

Disruptive voices are often champions for the change they bring about, advocating the benefits for the wider industry and the customer experience. Think of high-profile people such as Elon Musk. They not only innovate but lead from the front and vocally challenge convention at every turn.

With this in mind, Stephanie said it is not simply the act of producing a product or service that changes expectations and perceptions, but also being a leader and voice for change.

'To become a disruptor, you have to find something that you don't like about your industry and focus on changing it at whatever level you want, whether that is locally or nationally or internationally. But you've got to be willing to be vocal about the change you're making. You've got to be willing to call out what you're doing and why.'

Stephanie warns that this is also an approach which can prove divisive.

'This means that sometimes you're going to make enemies. You don't have to call out individual competitors, but you do have to be willing to stand up and say, "We don't agree with this as the norm in the industry, so we're doing things differently.'"

REVOLUTIONIZING AN INDUSTRY

One traditional sector that has been radically overhauled in recent years is the education industry and, like most things, the speed of that change has increased rapidly due to the fallout from the COVID-19 pandemic.

It is doubtful that most parents would have utilized technology in their children's educations prior to 2020, when schools around the world were forced to curtail their regular teaching practices and introduce alternatives such as remote online learning.

But while this may have sped up the rollout of tech-based educational solutions, as with concepts such as flexible working, the building blocks were already in place.

The term 'edtech' is an abbreviation of 'educational technology' – essentially the practice of using apps and software to facilitate learning.

Before co-founding edtech company NewCampus, Singapore-based Australian entrepreneur Fei Yao worked in a variety of roles around the world, including with Engineers Without Borders on an innovative water purification project in Cambodia, and as a management consultant at Accenture in Australia.

The company is billed as a lifelong learning school for professionals. The instructors are global entrepreneurs who are live-streamed into small group classes.

The curriculum focuses on topics that prepare people for a changing world, including emerging technologies, trending industries and digital skills, and NewCampus offers live workshops, masterclasses and virtual conferences.

Her work in the field has been recognized by Forbes 30 Under 30 and has seen her named among AmCham Shanghai Future Leaders of the Year and CMO Asia Top 50 Women Leaders.

'Disrupting a market to me means shifting the fundamental attitudes and behaviours of a segment of users,' says Fei.

Once again with the concept of disruption we return to the concept of shifting customers' expectations. In this context, disruption is not about deploying a clever piece of tech that allows you to overtake a competitor. It goes deeper than that: it is about changing the perceptions of people, perceptions that may have been ingrained for decades or even centuries. It is about redefining what is possible.

She says: 'It's not really disruptive if your users are people who are choosing you over a competitor, but it becomes very interesting if your users are people who have never engaged with your type of product.

'At NewCampus we're most excited by the more mature students who have been in stable jobs for a long time after a previously "reliable" degree but have dramatically changed their view on the place of education in the career.'

So again in this context, the disruption is not just about NewCampus developing a new offering that allows it to compete with existing educational institutions. Just as was true for Airbnb, the disruption redraws the boundaries – of what further education is and where it is delivered, for both customers and the wider market. Customers are drawn to it over more traditional or established competitors, and their perception of what education is and what it can help them achieve has been altered.

Many traditional educational institutions were already observing how the edtech sector was shifting these boundaries. The pace of change has only been sped up by the pandemic, with these traditional institutions having to adopt new ways of doing things, methods which have been pioneered by new start-ups with technology at their core.

As we move towards a new era of tech-based learning, these traditional institutions face the prospect of either having to adopt some of these new methods or be left behind. And once again, that is the very definition of disrupting an industry.

GEOGRAPHIC CHALLENGES

Despite the opportunities afforded by tech and new ways of doing things, being a disruptor still comes with potential hurdles.

Fei's business is based in Singapore, which has presented its own challenges. Although it is a forward-looking and respected centre of tech and entrepreneurship in Asia, the city is not as well-known as an educational centre of excellence compared to traditional university cities such as Oxford and Cambridge.

But by challenging expectations, Fei says that NewCampus is disrupting people's expectations, not just in terms of how they're educated – but where.

'Higher education has always been a luxury brand.

'And like other luxury brands, products from Europe and the US are perceived to be of better quality.

'So our challenge in building a business education brand with a global-first lens from Asia is challenging a longstanding perception in the market. But it is also an exciting, and timely challenge!'

TAKING THE TRADITIONALISTS WITH YOU

Making a big impression with a disruptive offering and being a vocal advocate for change can alter how the traditional big players operate.

As you redraw customer and market expectations and ways of doing things, more traditional operators in that world have a number of choices.

They can:
- do nothing;
- try to adopt your technology and compete with you;
- buy you out;
- work with you.

In the last decade there has been a scramble by some of the world's largest financial institutions to invest in fintech start-ups. One of the reasons was that they saw the opportunity to acquire tech that was already proven.

It is not just in banking circles, though, that relationships between traditional operators and disruptive start-ups are being forged to the benefit of both parties.

This was the case with Olio when it came to partner with a major British retailer.

Saasha Celestial-One says, 'I think being a disruptor means [asking this]: if successful and once at scale, will the industry within which you're operating look the same or fundamentally different?

'If we can "flip" the decision-making process such that when people are sourcing food they look at Olio, a secondary market, to see what's going spare, before they head to the store (the primary market), then we'll have significantly disrupted that primary market …

'Thus, food retailers will have to evolve or reinvent themselves to stay competitive in what is already a fiercely competitive and low-margin business.

'Selling food cheaply, knowing a significant part of it will end up uneaten, will no longer be a competitive advantage.

'At Olio, we have thousands of volunteers collecting unsold food from [UKsupermarket] Tesco every week and redistributing it from their homes via Olio to their neighbours.

'Managing this is a paid-for service and forms an important part of our revenue.

'Tesco is a leader in this area – rather than fighting the disruption, they've figured that can partner with us and lead the disruption!

'In a recent survey of 4000+ Olioers, 63 per cent said they will shop more at Tesco if they can as a result of our food-waste fighting partnership. 'If you're looking to disrupt an industry, I think you need to find an anchor member of that industry, who can get on board and legitimize (rather than stall) your disruption.'

IDEA BEFORE TECH

Technology is what the disruptive sector uses to, well, disrupt!

With the cab company Uber, it is the Uber app that allows the service to facilitate the interaction between drivers and customers and direct vehicles to their pickups.

But while the technology enabled Uber to disrupt the industry, the genesis of the company itself was not the tech – but the desire to change something. The company's founders first identified a need, something missing, which they felt their technology could overcome.

With that in mind, for an entrepreneur who wants to disrupt a sector, the idea – and the passion – must come first; the tech comes later. Otherwise, the venture itself could fall flat. When it comes to being a disruptor, Fei says that you must first identify the need and how you are going to fulfil that need, then get involved in the industry and make contacts. After that, apply the tech, and let the disruption begin.

Fei advises:
- Fall in love with the problem, not the solution. Your product and solution will need to change as the market changes, but if your users have a problem and a need to solve this problem, you can always adapt what you are building.
- Building a company is always going to be hard, but it does not have to be lonely. Surround yourself with good people who are moving in a similar direction, so that you can lean on them for support when you need it. Like your solution ideas, your problems are probably not unique. Find a support group, so you can share your problems and grow together.

She adds: 'We've seen the first wave of edtech use technology as a tool to enhance learning with mostly disappointing results.

'It mostly involved throwing content online and augmenting the experience with quizzes and forums.

'My advice would be to focus on the education first, and the technology second. I believe in edtech, pedagogy is technology – it doesn't matter how good the platform is if the learning isn't happening.'

She concludes: 'Education hasn't had much of an incentive to change up until now, but this means there is a limitless opportunity ahead to continuously improve how people learn in the continuously changing world ahead.'

CONCLUSIONS

Sun Tzu spoke about the importance of being first to the battlefield, which means that the army will be more prepared, more settled and much more ready to engage in battle. The army which arrives second will be off balance, in haste and on the back foot.

In a related point, he also spoke about imposing your will on the enemy and making them dance to your tune.

There are two clear lessons here for entrepreneurs:

■ Be a first mover.

■ Companies that are first with a product or service can gain significant advantages. It allows them to set prices, refine their processes and establish brand loyalty, which can last a considerable amount of time. From Amazon to Coca-Cola, being first can lead to big things.

■ The power of disruption.

■ We live in an age of disruption. From Uber and Airbnb, to the countless millions of start-up companies in fintech, edtech and other sectors, entrepreneurs are revolutionizing industries that have remained set in their ways for decades and even centuries. Being able to do this requires passion, ideas and originality, as well as an enterprising entrepreneur ready to be a vocal and persuasive advocate of change.

Weak Points and Strong

(Sun Tzu's Original Text)

1. Sun Tzu said: Whoever is first in the field and awaits the coming of the enemy, will be fresh for the fight; whoever is second in the field and has to hasten to battle will arrive exhausted.

2. Therefore the clever combatant imposes his will on the enemy, but does not allow the enemy's will to be imposed on him.

3. By holding out advantages to him, he can cause the enemy to approach of his own accord; or, by inflicting damage, he can make it impossible for the enemy to draw near.

4. If the enemy is taking his ease, he can harass him; if well supplied with food, he can starve him out; if quietly encamped, he can force him to move.

5. Appear at points which the enemy must hasten to defend; march swiftly to places where you are not expected.

6. An army may march great distances without distress, if it marches through country where the enemy is not.

7. You can be sure of succeeding in your attacks if you only attack places which are undefended. You can ensure the safety of your defence if you only hold positions that cannot be attacked.

8. Hence that general is skilful in attack whose opponent does not know what to defend; and he is skilful in defence whose opponent does not know what to attack.

9. O divine art of subtlety and secrecy! Through you we learn to be invisible, through you inaudible; and hence we can hold the enemy's fate in our hands.

10. You may advance and be absolutely irresistible, if you make for the enemy's weak points; you may retire and be safe from pursuit if your movements are more rapid than those of the enemy.

11. If we wish to fight, the enemy can be forced to an engagement even though he be sheltered behind a high rampart and a deep ditch. All we need do is attack some other place that he will be obliged to relieve.

12. If we do not wish to fight, we can prevent the enemy from engaging us even though the lines of our encampment be merely traced out on the ground. All we need do is to throw something odd and unaccountable in his way.

13. By discovering the enemy's dispositions and remaining invisible ourselves, we can keep our forces concentrated, while the enemy's must be divided.

14. We can form a single united body, while the enemy must split up into fractions. Hence there will be a whole pitted against separate parts of a whole, which means that we shall be many to the enemy's few.

15. And if we are able thus to attack an inferior force with a superior one, our opponents will be in dire straits.

16. The spot where we intend to fight must not be made known; for then the enemy will have to prepare against a possible attack at several different points; and his forces being thus distributed in many directions, the numbers we shall have to face at any given point will be proportionately few.

17. For should the enemy strengthen his van, he will weaken his rear; should he strengthen his rear, he will weaken his van; should he strengthen his left, he will weaken

his right; should he strengthen his right, he will weaken his left. If he sends reinforcements everywhere, he will everywhere be weak.

18. Numerical weakness comes from having to prepare against possible attacks; numerical strength, from compelling our adversary to make these preparations against us.

19. Knowing the place and the time of the coming battle, we may concentrate from the greatest distances in order to fight.

20. But if neither time nor place be known, then the left wing will be impotent to succour the right, the right equally impotent to succour the left, the van unable to relieve the rear, or the rear to support the van. How much more so if the furthest portions of the army are anything under a hundred *li* apart, and even the nearest are separated by several *li*!

21. Though according to my estimate the soldiers of Yueh exceed our own in number, that shall advantage them nothing in the matter of victory. I say then that victory can be achieved.

22. Though the enemy be stronger in numbers, we may prevent him from fighting. Scheme so as to discover his plans and the likelihood of their success.

23. Rouse him, and learn the principle of his activity or inactivity. Force him to reveal himself, so as to find out his vulnerable spots.

24. Carefully compare the opposing army with your own, so that you may know where strength is superabundant and where it is deficient.

25. In making tactical dispositions, the highest pitch you can attain is to conceal them; conceal your dispositions, and you will be safe from the prying of the subtlest spies, from the machinations of the wisest brains.

26. How victory may be produced for them out of the enemy's own tactics – that is what the multitude cannot comprehend.

27. All men can see the tactics whereby I conquer, but what none can see is the strategy out of which victory is evolved.

28. Do not repeat the tactics which have gained you one victory, but let your methods be regulated by the infinite variety of circumstances.

29. Military tactics are like unto water; for water in its natural course runs away from high places and hastens downwards.

30. So in war, the way is to avoid what is strong and to strike at what is weak.

31. Water shapes its course according to the nature of the ground over which it flows; the soldier works out his victory in relation to the foe whom he is facing.

32. Therefore, just as water retains no constant shape, so in warfare there are no constant conditions.

33. He who can modify his tactics in relation to his opponent and thereby succeed in winning, may be called a heaven-born captain.

34. The five elements (water, fire, wood, metal, earth) are not always equally predominant; the four seasons make way for each other in turn. There are short days and long; the moon has its periods of waning and waxing.

CHAPTER 7

MANOEUVRING

Much of Sun Tzu's teachings relate to the importance of preparedness, be it in the organization of forces, intelligence gathering, or understanding your own strengths and weaknesses. But all the preparation in the world would be for nothing if the army itself did not do what it was supposed to do once battle was joined. Plans may lay the foundations for victory, but armies win battles.

In this chapter, Sun Tzu talked about instilling order and organization so an army was ready and able to respond to the general's commands. He taught that how an army is formed and held together – such as how generals, officers and troops work in concert – is a central component of enabling the army to move properly and effectively.

Manoeuvring with an army is advantageous; with an undisciplined multitude, most dangerous.

Whether it is an army or a business organization, both rely on their component human beings as well as the relationships between those at every level of the organization. How they work together, how they pull together, how discipline is installed and how rewards are granted. How does everyone learn to pull in the same direction, and are they engaged with the company ethos? How do you ensure they are 'bought in' to the vision?

COORDINATING YOUR ARMY

Any organization is a combination of people, all with their own skills, abilities and roles. Success as an entrepreneur with employees is being able to ensure they work as one and respond to commands.

Stephanie Scheller has spoken widely on the subject in presentations to business and also built her own successful company. She says it is important to communicate vision to staff so that they feel invested in the company's future.

'One of the most important keys to creating a team that is moving in the same direction is clarity on your vision for what the company will look like long term, and ensuring you have communicated that vision clearly.

'Too often I work with business owners who have a goal for what they are building [which] hasn't been communicated to their team.

'Because we, as entrepreneurs, live and breathe with our goals and talk about them all the time to ourselves, we make the faulty assumption that our team knows it too.'

In order to do this correctly, Stephanie says there are two important points to bear in mind. These are:
- Know your goals in detail.
- Communicate that vision to the team, both when hiring and also in the longer term.

KEEPING STAFF IN THE LOOP

But how do we communicate our vision to staff and keep them onboard over the long term? After all, communication is a skill and something which not everyone is experienced in.

According to Stephanie, consistently sharing a vision and keeping people motivated has three key aspects.

A monthly team meeting

'I know, everyone hates these at most companies. But we've made it a fun, brainstorming opportunity where I update everyone on the overall evolution of the entire company and how things are updating from one division to the next.

'We discuss the challenges we're dealing with and the evolutions we're experiencing to the vision and mission, and I take everyone's input seriously.

'It's a protected space where you can speak up and share without worrying and everyone knows that.'

Regular one-on-ones

'These vary in frequency depending on how much guidance the team member needs. I have some people [meeting] weekly and some [meeting] monthly. But these are one of the key pivot points that allow me to:

- identify problems and help course correct the team member before they go too far off the path;
- identify challenges the team member is having (or might have down the road) and help them solve them proactively;
- communicate and connect on a personal level to keep engagement high.'

Project management transparency

'I complete an updated one-page-business-plan every year and share the plan with the team.

'This way they can see how the vision and mission has evolved in writing every year as well as see the goals we'll be working towards to make it happen. We have a project management board that everyone can see all aspects of, so they can see what we're working on, and when their projects are due!'

THE IMPORTANCE OF VISION

The word 'vision' is one of many that can be thrown around from time to time in business circles, but what does it really mean? Why is it important?

Organizations, like an army, are composed of individuals. They are part of a whole, and the success of that whole depends on how invested those individuals feel. A huge part of that is understanding what the overall goals are – even if they do not need to know the finer details.

An entrepreneur is passionate about what they do; it is the reason they do what they do – to be successful during business growth. It is therefore vital that they can convey to their employees why they feel that way, and what they hope the company is going to achieve.

Jeremy Stern, who has built PromoVeritas from the ground up, agrees wholeheartedly.

'There is a view that companies with a purpose are more successful than those without, or the ones that fail to get buy-in to their purpose from staff.

'At PromoVeritas, our mission and vision are printed in several places on the walls, and every new starter has a two-week induction plan with talks from me and others on the history of the company, our purpose, etc.

'It really does help with those first critical weeks and getting them on board.'

KEEPING PEOPLE ON TRACK

Of course, imbuing new recruits with the company's vision is easy enough, but how can we ensure staff remain true to the company's values?

Jeremy said the tricky bit comes if these efforts to embed the company's vision with staff do not stick.

'If more experienced staff forget about how to behave with clients [and] what our values are, mistakes start to occur.

'Getting people back on track is hard. Yes, we have computer systems and timesheets and process flows, but we also rely heavily on our people to do things right, first time. Double-checking everything is not an option and yet the price of failure can be significant.'

Like Stephanie, Jeremy also strongly advocates the idea of one-to-ones with staff.

Sometimes this has resulted in him having to take tough decisions for the good of the company.

'We attempt to deal with this [keeping people onboard] through a variety of means.

'Firstly, fortnightly one-to-ones with their line manager, backed up by six-monthly formal appraisals, and I read every one.

'If necessary there is a development plan, and this could lead to a letter of caution or a formal performance plan if improvements are still not forthcoming.

'And yes, ultimately, we have had to exit some staff who just did not want to work in the right way.

'But I have always found that other staff get it, they know the non-performers, the awkward ones, and whilst they may alert senior management to issues, they are grateful when the problem is sorted.'

NAVIGATING THE MARKETPLACE

As well as the ability of the army to manoeuvre through terrain, the terrain itself is also a prime factor in determining victory or defeat. Sun Tzu said that as well as being in control of their force, commanders should know what the terrain is like around them.

We are not fit to lead an army on the march unless we are familiar with the face of the country – its mountains and forests, its pitfalls and precipices, its marshes and swamps.

KNOWING THE MARKET TAKES CONSTANT VIGILANCE

We have talked about how to analyze the market before launching a new endeavour and the importance of knowing whether what you are offering is in demand.

But understanding the marketplace is a constant battle. It is absolutely vital that an entrepreneur stays plugged in to what is going on at all times. That is their terrain, their mountains, their rivers and their ravines.

We focused previously on the idea of using analytics and surveys and concepts such as top-down analysis, but for Stephanie there is a much more simple way of going about things: just ask!

'Doing interviews is the best way to analyze the market.

'Talk to the buyers, talk to the sellers.

'Ask the buyers what they love about the market and their provider, ask them what they hate about it. Ask them how much they would pay if that thing they hated would go away forever.

'Ask sellers what they love about their buyers, and what they hate. Ask them about the challenges of providing services and generating clients.'

CHOOSE YOUR ALLIES CAREFULLY

To enable a better understanding of the country, Sun Tzu also suggested using local guides and the building of alliances.

> ## We cannot enter into alliances until we are acquainted with the designs of our neighbours.

In a business context, alliances can take many forms. They could be simple business acquaintances or more formal agreements. There could be times, for example, where it is helpful to form a business relationship with someone who knows the market better than you do. By doing so, you gain a greater awareness of the terrain into which you are manoeuvring.

However, a huge amount of care should be taken when entering into any business relationship.

Stephanie has previously written in detail about the importance of the right type of friendships in business.

'I would say that you need to constantly be analyzing your network and the people you're hanging out with.

'Some of the people that got you to where you are, aren't going to be part of getting you to where you're going.

'This doesn't mean you have to be an ass and kick them out of your life, but you can slowly extract yourself from being around them consistently and be careful about how much of their perspective filters into your head.'

KNOWLEDGE AND ENERGY

Business relationships are often practical, forged out of a need to share information, insights and expertise. But like all relationships they have the potential to be both positive and negative. Stephanie said it is vital to recognize when those relationships become potentially damaging.

'When you find yourself hanging out with someone who brings you down, who (when you're done hanging out) leaves you feeling gritty and exhausted, or when you find that you've outpaced and outgrown them, it's time to move on.

'If you find yourself spending time around people who only ever dream and plot and plan but never take action, once you realize you're hanging out with someone who is a waste of time, move on.

'When you're forming a business relationship, especially with someone who is going to help you level up, you've got to be looking for what you can bring to the relationship that is valuable.

'If they aren't reciprocating, you can always move on to someone else, but start every relationship looking for ways to add value to the other person.'

BE SINCERE

Business relationships do not always have to revolve around a quid pro quo.

Being genuine will go a long way, with the potential for long-term benefits even if immediate payoffs are not yet apparent.

Stephanie says: 'Truly, honestly care about them as a person, not just what they can do for you. Trust me, when you are hanging out with someone who only sees you for what you can do for them, it makes you feel like a used Kleenex, and none of us like that feeling.'

RESEARCH YOUR ALLIES

It is vital to pick your allies carefully – and that involves research. There are many ways to do this, from simple Linkedin and internet searches to recommendations from business acquaintances and business organizations.

'There's definitely something to be said for doing research around a potential ally," says Stephanie. 'But at the same time, you don't need to go overboard and spend days and months and hire a private investigator to try and find out if the person has anything seedy about them.

'But when someone shows you their true colours, trust them the first time.

'The good news is, a simple Google Search will usually tell you if there's something to be wary of. At the end of the day, though, I'm a fan of having a very straightforward conversation with someone.

'If there's something potentially shady or concerning in their background, I like to ask them straight up about it and watch their response to decide if it's going to impact their future and whether I need to distance myself or not.'

TRUST YOUR INSTINCTS

Reputations can precede people in business, and there may be individuals who want to disrupt business relationships that have the potential to present a competitive challenge in the future. Stephanie's advice is that while it is okay to take advice, you should also trust your own instincts too.

'I like to take other people's advice about someone and consider it, but at the end of the day, draw my own conclusions, because people change.

'Obviously, if you're getting into bed with someone in the sense of becoming a partner or really becoming involved, then I recommend starting small.

'Don't make them a partner in the business right away. Start with designing a project that you can work on with them first and see how that goes.

'Then you can open discussion about becoming partners, but set landmarks to hit together to see if being partners would make sense before actually signing over part of your business.'

BREAKING THE ICE

Reaching out to potential allies is not always easy. Indeed, one of the many reasons some people choose to become entrepreneurs is because they like to fly solo and be masters of their own destiny. But there are still occasions where it becomes necessary to bite the bullet, go out there and make friends.

Joe Wehbe found that working on mutually beneficial projects with like-minded individuals was a great way to make that happen.

'I always like to use a door opener, something that does not have friction.

'Working on a collaborative book was a really low-friction way to connect with some like-minded people.

'It's also something that gives me more licence to reach out to other people I want to reach out to.

'Imagine someone you think of as "successful", who you look up to and would love to have a relationship with.

'How many people send them emails and messages with vague requests asking for advice or the chance to "meet up for a coffee"?

'It was much easier to reach out to them by saying: "I'm an author writing a book on advice to our 18-year-old-selves and would love to hear your thoughts on this topic – what key piece of advice would you give your younger self?"'

Like Stephanie, Joe also focuses on creating genuine friendships.

'When I focused on setting up good referral relationships with other mortgage brokers, accountants and lawyers, for instance, in real estate, I soon learned that the best connections come from people who you genuinely connect with.

'People you have less in common with and align with less aren't as likely to send business your way, and you're not as likely to send business in their direction!

'So, I have personally done away with the concept of "networking" – I find it more worthwhile, enjoyable and profitable to build genuine relationships and friendships that also have business utility and upside.'

CONCLUSIONS

Sun Tzu wrote about the importance of having a well-marshalled army to make it easier to manoeuvre. He also said that a vital aspect of manoeuvring was understanding the terrain around you. One way of gaining insights into that terrain was the use of alliances.

From a business perspective, there are lessons around the following:

■ Share your vision.

■ Having a strong vision for your business is crucial if you are going to be able to encourage buy-in from your employees.

■ Keep watching the market.
It is crucial to keep an eye on the market. That is your terrain, and it is always changing.

■ Pick your allies.
If you need to form business relationships, ensure you research these potential allies well. Be sincere and seek out mutual benefits.

Manoeuvring

(Sun Tzu's Original Text)

1. Sun Tzu said: In war, the general receives his commands from the sovereign.

2. Having collected an army and concentrated his forces, he must blend and harmonize the different elements thereof before pitching his camp.

3. After that, comes tactical manoeuvring, than which there is nothing more difficult. The difficulty of tactical manoeuvring consists in turning the devious into the direct, and misfortune into gain.

4. Thus, to take a long and circuitous route, after enticing the enemy out of the way, and though starting after him, to contrive to reach the goal before him, shows knowledge of the artifice of deviation.

5. Manoeuvring with an army is advantageous; with an undisciplined multitude, most dangerous.

6. If you set a fully equipped army in march in order to snatch an advantage, the chances are that you will be too late. On the other hand, to detach a flying column for the purpose involves the sacrifice of its baggage and stores.

CHAPTER 7

7. Thus, if you order your men to roll up their buff-coats, and make forced marches without halting day or night, covering double the usual distance at a stretch, doing a hundred *li* in order to wrest an advantage, the leaders of all your three divisions will fall into the hands of the enemy.

8. The stronger men will be in front, the jaded ones will fall behind, and on this plan only one-tenth of your army will reach its destination.

9. If you march fifty *li* in order to outmanoeuvre the enemy, you will lose the leader of your first division, and only half your force will reach the goal.

10. If you march thirty *li* with the same object, two-thirds of your army will arrive.

11. We may take it then that an army without its baggage-train is lost; without provisions it is lost; without bases of supply it is lost.

12. We cannot enter into alliances until we are acquainted with the designs of our neighbours.

13. We are not fit to lead an army on the march unless we are familiar with the face of the country – its mountains and forests, its pitfalls and precipices, its marshes and swamps.

14. We shall be unable to turn natural advantage to account unless we make use of local guides.

15. In war, practise dissimulation, and you will succeed.

16. Whether to concentrate or to divide your troops must be decided by circumstances.

17. Let your rapidity be that of the wind, your compactness be that of the forest.

18. In raiding and plundering be like fire, in immovability like a mountain.

19. Let your plans be dark and impenetrable as night, and when you move, fall like a thunderbolt.

20. When you plunder a countryside, let the spoil be divided amongst your men; when you capture new territory, cut it up into allotments for the benefit of the soldiery.

21. Ponder and deliberate before you make a move.

22. He will conquer who has learnt the artifice of deviation. Such is the art of manoeuvring.

23. The Book of Army Management says: On the field of battle, the spoken word does not carry far enough: hence the institution of gongs and drums. Nor can ordinary objects be seen clearly enough: hence the institution of banners and flags.

24. Gongs and drums, banners and flags, are means whereby the ears and eyes of the host may be focused on one particular point.

25. The host thus forming a single united body, it is impossible either for the brave to advance alone, or for the cowardly to retreat alone. This is the art of handling large masses of men.

26. In night-fighting, then, make much use of signal-fires and drums, and in fighting by day, of flags and banners, as a means of influencing the ears and eyes of your army.

27. A whole army may be robbed of its spirit; a commander-in-chief may be robbed of his presence of mind.

28. Now a soldier's spirit is keenest in the morning; by noonday it has begun to flag; and in the evening, his mind is bent only on returning to camp.

29. A clever general, therefore, avoids an army when its spirit is keen, but attacks it when it is sluggish and inclined to return. This is the art of studying moods.

30. Disciplined and calm, to await the appearance of disorder and hubbub amongst the enemy: – this is the art of retaining self-possession.

31. To be near the goal while the enemy is still far from it, to wait at ease while the enemy is toiling and struggling, to be well-fed while the enemy is famished: – this is the art of husbanding one's strength.

32. To refrain from intercepting an enemy whose banners are in perfect order, to refrain from attacking an army drawn up in calm and confident array: – this is the art of studying circumstances.

33. It is a military axiom not to advance uphill against the enemy, nor to oppose him when he comes downhill.

34. Do not pursue an enemy who simulates flight; do not attack soldiers whose temper is keen.

35. Do not swallow bait offered by the enemy. Do not interfere with an army that is returning home.

36. When you surround an army, leave an outlet free. Do not press a desperate foe too hard.

37. Such is the art of warfare.

CHAPTER 8

VARIATION IN TACTICS

Sun Tzu believed that being able to adapt tactics to meet a particular goal was crucial to victory. The actions of an enemy, or the weather, or physical conditions on a battlefield, are in a state of constant flux, and all require a response. The same is true for markets and the actions of business rivals.

Sun Tzu believed there were five dangerous faults that might affect a general:
■ recklessness, which leads to destruction;
■ cowardice, which leads to capture;
■ a hasty temper, which can be provoked by insults;
■ a delicacy of honour, which is sensitive to shame;
■ oversolicitude for the soldiers, leading to worry and trouble.

A great business leader, like an effective general, must take time to make rational decisions but also be bold in their execution. They should also be able to maintain a healthy separation from themselves and the staff under them in order to remain objective.

BE WARY OF THE WRONG MOVE
When trying to make progress in any endeavour, knowing which routes not to take is at least as important as knowing which routes to take.

There are roads which must not be followed, armies which must not be attacked, towns which must not be besieged, positions which must not be contested, commands of the sovereign which must not be obeyed.

As well as being decisive when pursuing a new venture, it is important to be decisive when knowing when to change course.

This is something Joe Wehbe says he has learned during his time as an entrepreneur.

'To be honest, I think my best examples of decisiveness have been in knowing when to pull the plug on something. A key example was shutting down a non-profit, From the Ground Up – a decision made in 2018.'

This early venture of Joe's began in response to the Nepal earthquake of 2015, which devastated the country.

Joe began the organization using his friend's building skills to work with a small community on restoration and improving public infrastructure such as schools and a health centre.

Joe's associate established a construction company at the same time and before long, it became apparent that they would have to choose which project to pursue.

'So we developed a split focus between the non-profit work we'd started out doing and had won social approval for (building schools, most specifically) and the much more sustainable and high-impact business project (construction and manufacturing).

'It's not always an easy decision to make, but in most situations it makes sense to double-down on the one area that is delivering the most value than spreading oneself thin over a range of services or products. It also made sense to only do what we could be doing uniquely.'

So after some deliberation, they decided to shut down the non-profit part of their work in order to focus on the impactful business.

'I'll be honest, this decision removed a role I really loved doing, but to me, this was success on my terms – putting the "customer" (in this case, stakeholders in Nepal, and the industry) first.

'Let's be honest, I've been indecisive way more times than I've shown clarity and conviction. But this is an example of it working out, in a not-so-obvious version of success.'

Carla Williams Johnson agrees with Joe's principle:

'This may be hard for some people to admit, but I see it regularly where people are continuously pumping funds into an avenue that's not helping their business grow.

'At this point, it's no longer an investment but an expense and you have to be able to walk away.'

THE IMPORTANCE OF BUDGETING

The bottom line will often tell you if you are heading down the wrong path. A business venture that is not profitable will be a waste of time and resources, and also expend your physical and mental energy – energy which could be better invested in more profitable endeavours.

Having limits on what you are prepared to spend on these ventures, and having a 'red line' you are not prepared to cross, is a good way of ensuring you do not stray too far down the wrong path. But even that is not always so straightforward.

Stephanie Scheller says: 'Budgeting is incredibly important in one aspect and can be a problem in another! Part of that budgeting that matters so much is ensuring you're charging enough to cover costs, marketing, payroll, and still make a profit!

'It's also extremely important to make sure you're not overcommitting on your recurring expenses and finding yourself underwater or with such a large monthly recurring expense amount that you can't think straight to get on top of it.

'Where I think budgeting becomes a problem is when we end up married to the budget and pouring hours and hours into budgeting and projections.

'Instead of sitting there with spreadsheet after spreadsheet projecting how much money you think you're going to make, get out there and actually start working on making it!

'I think we end up sending good money after bad a lot because we get married to the sunk cost and think that we're going to get it to turn a corner.

'This is the challenge with entrepreneurs. We are eternal optimists so we are always "just about to make it big ...", but so often we don't recognize when we're really screwed and nothing has changed to make the next investment actually make money.'

To avoid this, Stephanie advises taking into account the following points:

■ Whenever you are starting a project, establish the line you are not willing to cross financially before you get into the project.

■ 'It's so hard to back up once you're in the thick of it. But if you tell yourself: "You know what, I'm not willing to lose more than $10k or $20K" and then track it, this also forces you to have the honest and challenging conversation with yourself about how to maximize return and limit the bleeding that is the destruction of so many businesses.'

■ Work with a coach who knows the maximum you will invest and is watching out for that figure, because it can be difficult to reset that barrier once you are in the thick of it.

■ Participate in a business mastermind or group, who can call you out impartially if they feel you are getting in too deep.

■ 'They will also usually be better at pointing out if you're living the definition of insanity and expecting that somehow you're going to get a different result when you're doing the same thing over and over even if you think things are different. [Things] often aren't, but it's really hard for us to see that sometimes.'

CONCLUSIONS

In this chapter, Sun Tzu spoke of the importance of not making the wrong move. Roads that must not be followed and roads that must not be attacked.

In a business context, this is all about the importance of not pursuing the wrong goals, and of also being decisive enough to change course if things are not going to plan. You should:

■ Have a financial 'red line' you are not prepared to cross when persevering with a project or goal.

■ Have allies/friends who are prepared to tell you when you are throwing good money after bad.

■ Remember that changing course is not failure.

Variation in Tactics

(Sun Tzu's Original Text)

1. Sun Tzu said: In war, the general receives his commands from the sovereign, collects his army and concentrates his forces.

2. When in difficult country, do not encamp. In country where high roads intersect, join hands with your allies. Do not linger in dangerously isolated positions. In hemmed-in situations, you must resort to stratagem. In desperate positions, you must fight.

3. There are roads which must not be followed, armies which must not be attacked, towns which must not be besieged, positions which must not be contested, commands of the sovereign which must not be obeyed.

4. The general who thoroughly understands the advantages that accompany variation of tactics knows how to handle his troops.

5. The general who does not understand these, may be well acquainted with the configuration of the country, yet he will not be able to turn his knowledge to practical account.

CHAPTER 8

6. So, the student of war who is unversed in the art of war of varying his plans, even though he be acquainted with the Five Advantages, will fail to make the best use of his men.

7. Hence in the wise leader's plans, considerations of advantage and of disadvantage will be blended together.

8. If our expectation of advantage be tempered in this way, we may succeed in accomplishing the essential part of our schemes.

9. If, on the other hand, in the midst of difficulties we are always ready to seize an advantage, we may extricate ourselves from misfortune.

10. Reduce the hostile chiefs by inflicting damage on them; and make trouble for them, and keep them constantly engaged; hold out specious allurements, and make them rush to any given point.

11. The art of war teaches us to rely not on the likelihood of the enemy's not coming, but on our own readiness to receive him; not on the chance of his not attacking, but rather on the fact that we have made our position unassailable.

12. There are five dangerous faults which may affect a general:
    (1) Recklessness, which leads to destruction;
    (2) cowardice, which leads to capture;
    (3) a hasty temper, which can be provoked by insults;
    (4) a delicacy of honour which is sensitive to shame;
    (5) over-solicitude for his men, which exposes him to worry and trouble.

13. These are the five besetting sins of a general, ruinous to the conduct of war.

14. When an army is overthrown and its leader slain, the cause will surely be found among these five dangerous faults. Let them be a subject of meditation.

CHAPTER 9

THE ARMY ON THE MARCH

The army on the march may be required to do extraordinary things in order to secure tactical and strategic objectives.

An army can be likened to a company's workforce, no matter how big or small that workforce may be.

A business's ability to achieve its goals in the marketplace relies not only on the skills and abilities of that workforce, but also on their willingness to carry out their tasks.

In this chapter, Sun Tzu spoke of the importance of discipline in the ranks, but wisely stated that it is impossible to enforce discipline through the imposition of sanctions alone. The army must also be devoted to the leader imposing that discipline.

Conversely, he says that having the devotion of the soldiers but refusing to discipline them when the need arises, means they will become useless on the battlefield. He explained: 'If soldiers are punished before they have grown attached to you, they will not prove submissive; and, unless submissive, they will be practically useless.

If, when the soldiers have become attached to you, punishments are not enforced, they will still be useless.'

Therefore, soldiers must be treated in the first instance with humanity but kept under control by means of iron discipline. This is a certain road to victory.

CREATING A HAPPY WORKFORCE

As Sun Tzu spoke of engaging staff, creating loyalty and enforcing discipline, so must an entrepreneur do the same with their expanding workforce.

This may not always come easy for some entrepreneurs who have striven to get away from bureaucratic organizations and who might not wish to be seen as an enforcer of rules. But just as an army cannot function without discipline, nor can an organization – and Sun Tzu argued that discipline could not be properly instilled without devotion and loyalty first.

REWARDING STAFF

Jeremy Stern's company has grown significantly in recent years and one of the things he has endeavoured to do is keep his staff happy. Rewarding staff is a big part of that.

'Obviously, we seek to pay a fair salary and we do benchmark with other companies.

'We aim to be in the mid-range but then offer an enhanced package of benefits, so things like 27 days of holidays plus bank [public] holidays, a subsidized private health scheme, onsite parking and a bi-annual bonus that is linked to both the company performance and your own individual performance via the appraisal score.'

FINDING A BALANCE

According to Jeremy, it is also not quite as simple as paying a high wage because in a sales-based position where bonuses are part of the reward setup, this can lead to what he calls the 'wrong type' of behaviour.

'For a mid-manager, with the company hitting target and them getting an 8/10 appraisal score, the half year bonus would be about £4,000.

'This was a level we find motivating but not so much that it drives the wrong sort of sales aggressive behaviour that can be damaging to long-term client relationships.'

GOING DEEPER

But many people want more from their careers than just a wage and, like so many other aspects of our working lives, the pandemic has simply sped up what were already emerging trends.

Even before the upheaval wrought by Covid, millennials especially cited things such as work-life balance and believing in the goals and values of the company as being imperative when it comes both to applying to work somewhere and staying there.

The cost of hiring and training new staff means it is good practice for an employer to retain their workers, rather than constantly have to look for new ones.

PromoVeritas has a 'social monkeys' team which organizes monthly events. Before the pandemic hit, this included things such as bowling, games in the park or a day at Henley Regatta. As things eventually return to normal, companies will once again have the opportunity to reward staff in ways that go beyond simply paying them a wage.

Jeremy says: 'We try to have fun but are mindful that it means different things to different people and also of the tax implications for most such activities!'

Just as the pandemic pressed the accelerator for physical work changes such as the move to more remote working, so too has it heightened the desire people now have to feel more satisfied with their working lives.

A survey by recruitment company Robert Walters[1] found that 75 per

---

1   https://www.robertwalters.co.uk/content/dam/robert-walters/country/united-kingdom/files/whitepapers/the-future-of-work.pdf

cent of employees wanted their leaders to be more mindful of the need for staff work/life balance, while 53 per cent said they wanted management to have a better understanding of mental health and wellbeing.

The direction of travel is clear and the speed of that change has increased. Now more than ever, employees want to feel valued, be happy and to enjoy forms of fulfilment which lie outside the simple exchange of labour for pay.

COMMUNICATE

As we discussed earlier, the entrepreneur will always remain the centre of a growing organization, and establishing a strong bond with staff requires constantly extolling the virtues of what they are trying to achieve.

Building her edtech business, Fei Yao says that she made mistakes when it came to establishing and running a workforce – learning the hard way the importance of keeping her vision central to how the company runs.

'There is no such thing as over-communication. This also couldn't be more true in the era of remote work.

'This can be applied at all levels.

'Selling your vision to your team and selling your vision to your customers, investors and other stakeholders.'

DON'T BE AFRAID OF HYPE

In a world awash with social media and where start-ups are always looking to attract attention, Fei says there is absolutely nothing wrong with being your own cheerleader and that this will help align staff with your vision.

'It takes a village to raise a child, and we believe it takes a team to raise a start-up. Our people grow with us to take on more responsibility and ownership in the company.

'We live in a very crowded and noisy era. You have to be your own hype man or woman to remind people of what you do and why you do it, and that includes your team.

'Your team will feed off your energy and it's important to remind them why they are here.

'I have definitely made the mistake of giving managers too much autonomy and flexibility prematurely – and not circling back on the key vision and strategy.

'This just caused confusion and morale decline instead of ownership as I had hoped. Keep them updated with what feels like minor/trivial updates – it'll make a world of difference in keeping on the same page.'

THE IMPORTANCE OF DISCIPLINE

For anyone who remembers school or who dreams of leaving a company with strict policies and procedures, the idea of discipline may seem anathema, especially to those many entrepreneurs for whom freedom of expression is often of major importance.

But discipline in any organization is an essential component to ensure that it operates effectively. Bad discipline can radiate out and breed more misbehaviour or bad practice. It can also undermine trust from staff who do abide by the rules, as well as create an unpleasant place to work.

Each country will have its own employment laws that will determine how discipline can be enforced, but there are some common threads of good discipline. These are:

■ Have clear policies and procedures.
It is unfair to take punitive measures if someone does not know the rules. A company, regardless of its size, should have clearly defined rules about what is acceptable – whether it is uniform, behaviour in the office, or being late with deliverables. The rules should be written down, and all existing employees and new starters should have to sign to ensure they have been made aware of them. They should be made aware not only of the rules but of the cost of breaking those rules.

■ Give feedback.
It should not always be necessary to go straight to drastic punitive

measures. Instead, there should be other ways of dealing with breaches before it gets to that stage. You can have a 'sliding scale' of measures, which can begin with something as simple as having a chat in a relaxed environment. If this does not work, a more formal situation such as an office discussion with an HR representative present can be considered.

■ Follow a 'three strikes' rule.
This is something many companies adopt. Essentially, the employee gets several chances to mend their ways before disciplinary measures are taken. The form of those disciplinary measures is, of course, down to the individual entrepreneur.

WORD SPREADS

Do bear in mind, however, that as well as sometimes needing to be firm, it is equally important to be fair. In today's world, it is easy for employees to review their company online.

If they feel it is an unpleasant place to work or that punitive measures are dealt out too freely, they may not only feel unhappy. They may also potentially dissuade prospective future employees from wanting to work for you. Be fair to people – and more often than not, they will respond positively.

LAST RESORT

If a company is a happy ship, if due diligence is paid to recruitment or vetting, if clear feedback is provided to staff and they are onboard with the company's mission – in that case, disciplinary measures should not even be needed.

Arun Kapil says: 'I'm quite old school in terms of discipline mixed with a very liberal sprinkling of free-thinking.

'I'm a child of the '70s who grew up in the '90s summer(s) of love. I believe trust forms the basis of everything and if disciplinary procedures are needed, then the relationship is already over.

'It may sound trite, but we're a small team and so rely on each other to bring the best, much in the same way a family does.'

CONCLUSIONS

Sun Tzu talked of the army on the march and the commander's relationship to it. He spoke of the need to instil discipline, but also recognized that discipline would not be effective without first establishing devotion and loyalty.

In a business context, there are several important lessons to take from this.

■ Reward staff.
This is not simply about money, but could include things like social outings and staff rewards, flexible working or other practices that make your business a happy place to work.

■ Communicate.
This is an important part of building a workforce. They must feel invested, but also must be aware of the consequences of transgressions.

■ Discipline is important.
This may not always come easy, but there must be clear repercussions for transgressions, or else cohesion of the wider workforce can be threatened.

The Army on the March

(Sun Tzu's Original Text)

1. Sun Tzu said: We come now to the question of encamping the army, and observing signs of the enemy. Pass quickly over mountains, and keep in the neighbourhood of valleys.

2. Camp in high places, facing the sun. Do not climb heights in order to fight. So much for mountain warfare.

3. After crossing a river, you should get far away from it.

4. When an invading force crosses a river in its onward march, do not advance to meet it in mid-stream. It will be best to let half the army get across, and then deliver your attack.

5. If you are anxious to fight, you should not go to meet the invader near a river which he has to cross.

6. Moor your craft higher up than the enemy, and facing the sun. Do not move up-stream to meet the enemy. So much for river warfare.

7. In crossing salt-marshes, your sole concern should be to get over them quickly, without any delay.

8. If forced to fight in a salt-marsh, you should have water and grass near you, and get your back to a clump of trees. So much for operations in salt-marshes.

9. In dry, level country, take up an easily accessible position with rising ground to your right and on your rear, so that the danger may be in front, and safety lie behind. So much for campaigning in flat country.

10. These are the four useful branches of military knowledge which enabled the Yellow Emperor to vanquish four other sovereigns.

11. All armies prefer high ground to low and sunny places to dark.

12. If you are careful of your men, and camp on hard ground, the army will be free from disease of every kind, and this will spell victory.

13. When you come to a hill or a bank, occupy the sunny side, with the slope on your right rear. Thus you will at once act for the benefit of your soldiers and utilize the natural advantages of the ground.

14. When, in consequence of heavy rains up-country, a river which you wish to ford is swollen and flecked with foam, you must wait until it subsides.

15. Country in which there are precipitous cliffs with torrents running between, deep natural hollows, confined places, tangled thickets, quagmires and crevasses, should be left with all possible speed and not approached.

16. While we keep away from such places, we should get the enemy to approach them; while we face them, we should let the enemy have them on his rear.

17. If in the neighbourhood of your camp there should be any hilly country, ponds surrounded by aquatic grass, hollow basins filled with reeds, or woods with thick undergrowth, they must be carefully routed out and searched; for these are places where men in ambush or insidious spies are likely to be lurking.

18. When the enemy is close at hand and remains quiet, he is relying on the natural strength of his position.

19. When he keeps aloof and tries to provoke a battle, he is anxious for the other side to advance.

20. If his place of encampment is easy of access, he is tendering a bait.

21. Movement amongst the trees of a forest shows that the enemy is advancing. The appearance of a number of screens in the midst of thick grass means that the enemy wants to make us suspicious.

22. The rising of birds in their flight is the sign of an ambuscade. Startled beasts indicate that a sudden attack is coming.

23. When there is dust rising in a high column, it is the sign of chariots advancing; when the dust is low, but spread over a wide area, it betokens the approach of infantry. When it branches out in different directions, it shows that parties have been sent to collect firewood. A few clouds of dust moving to and fro signify that the army is encamping.

24. Humble words and increased preparations are signs that the enemy is about to advance. Violent language and driving forward as if to the attack are signs that he will retreat.

25. When the light chariots come out first and take up a position on the wings, it is a sign that the enemy is forming for battle.

26. Peace proposals unaccompanied by a sworn covenant indicate a plot.

27. When there is much running about and the soldiers fall into rank, it means that the critical moment has come.

28. When some are seen advancing and some retreating, it is a lure.

29. When the soldiers stand leaning on their spears, they are faint from want of food.

30. If those who are sent to draw water begin by drinking themselves, the army is suffering from thirst.

31. If the enemy sees an advantage to be gained and makes no effort to secure it, the soldiers are exhausted.

32. If birds gather on any spot, it is unoccupied. Clamour by night betokens nervousness.

33. If there is disturbance in the camp, the general's authority is weak. If the banners and flags are shifted about, sedition is afoot. If the officers are angry, it means that the men are weary.

34. When an army feeds its horses with grain and kills its cattle for food, and when the men do not hang their cooking-pots over the camp-fires, showing that they will not return to their tents, you may know that they are determined to fight to the death.

35. The sight of men whispering together in small knots or speaking in subdued tones points to disaffection amongst the rank and file.

36. Too frequent rewards signify that the enemy is at the end of his resources; too many punishments betray a condition of dire distress.

37. To begin by bluster, but afterwards to take fright at the enemy's numbers, shows a supreme lack of intelligence.

38. When envoys are sent with compliments in their mouths, it is a sign that the enemy wishes for a truce.

39. If the enemy's troops march up angrily and remain facing ours for a long time without either joining battle or taking themselves off again, the situation is one that demands great vigilance and circumspection.

40. If our troops are no more in number than the enemy, that is amply sufficient; it only means that no direct attack can be made. What we can do is simply to concentrate all our available strength, keep a close watch on the enemy, and obtain reinforcements.

41. He who exercises no forethought but makes light of his opponents is sure to be captured by them.

42. If soldiers are punished before they have grown attached to you, they will not prove submissive; and, unless submissive, they will be practically useless. If, when the soldiers have become attached to you, punishments are not enforced, they will still be useless.

43. Therefore soldiers must be treated in the first instance with humanity, but kept under control by means of iron discipline. This is a certain road to victory.

44. If in training soldiers commands are habitually enforced, the army will be well-disciplined; if not, its discipline will be bad.

45. If a general shows confidence in his men but always insists on his orders being obeyed, the gain will be mutual.

CHAPTER 10

TERRAIN

Sun Tzu touched on terrain in his discussions around manoeuvring, and used this chapter to expand on the issue in greater detail.

In the previous chapter, Sun Tzu spoke of the army on the march as something that was within a commander's control. It was within their ability to organize and to instil discipline, to ensure that the army was ready to meet the challenges presented by a rival – or, in a business context, a competitor.

The other principal component of any battle, beyond that of two or more armies, is terrain. The armies must move through terrain – and their actions are restricted or enabled by the quirks of that terrain.

Sun Tzu speaks of six different types of terrain:
- accessible ground;
- entangling ground;
- temporizing ground;
- narrow passes;
- precipitous heights;
- positions at a great distance from the enemy.

In the context of combat, the army and terrain are the two principal components. In the context of business, these are the company, which is made up of people and their various skills, and the market.

The market, and the various forces impacting on it at any given time, is the terrain through which the army of business must manoeuvre.

The crucial point to understand from Sun Tzu's perspective is that while one of these components – the army/business – may be something that a leader can exert control over, the terrain/market is not, on the face of it, so easily controlled.

But while the commander may not be able to change the terrain, they can choose where to move through that terrain. They can assess it and decide where and when to traverse it. They also know that what is an advantage/disadvantage for them is the same for a rival. By understanding that terrain, they can turn it to their advantage.

The same can be said for the market. While fluctuations, world events, pricing and the actions of rivals may alter that market, the business seeking to enter it or to capture a bigger share of it is not powerless in the face of those changes. Likewise, it behoves a wise commander and business leader to know when the market is not right to enter.

THE WRONG MARKET

Coffee giant Starbucks is without doubt one of the most recognizable brands on the planet with over 31,000 stores in 76 countries. It is a truly global brand (Shanghai alone has 256 Starbucks stores). Despite this global powerhouse's experience, expertise and financial power, it has been unable to crack the Australian market.

In 2008, Starbucks announced that it was closing two thirds of its stores Down Under, with fewer than 40 remaining across its vast land mass.

Many reasons have been suggested for Starbucks' failure to replicate its worldwide success in this market. One which carries some weight is the existing loyalty that many Australian customers have to their own local coffee shops.

The Antipodean nation has long had a thriving outdoor coffee culture, with coffee shops being as popular as the local pub thanks to the influx of Greek and Italian immigrants who brought coffee culture with them. The coffee industry in Australia was worth an estimated US $6 billion a year in 2018 – not bad for a population of fewer than 25 million.

The long-standing appreciation of coffee in the country meant that, in addition to having existing loyalty to particular shops, many Australians have also developed an experienced palate, often enjoying bespoke coffees available only in their town or city or even made to order. Observers noted that Starbucks, a well-oiled machine with very specific offerings and a set menu, was unable to cater for this degree of nuance.

Another reason for Starbucks's struggles may be that it launched too quickly and did not give Australian consumers time to get used to the brand and develop any affinity for it.

The implications in this context were clear. While Starbucks had its 'army' fully functioning and ready for action, the terrain – the market – was unforgiving. By contrast, its opponents – the local coffee shops – knew it well and used its nuances to their advantage.

YOUR ARMY AND YOUR TERRAIN

We talked earlier about ways to analyze the market, both before entering it and also when established (see page 17). Techniques include data analysis as well as questionnaires.

What is important also is to ensure a constant understanding of your organization's place in that market too. Just as Sun Tzu talked in separate terms about the army on the march (the business) and the terrain (the market), so too is it important to view both in a holistic sense. Stephanie Scheller reminds us that the two go very much hand in hand.

'If you understand your business and your model, pricing, fulfilment, sales, marketing, etc, in a way that works, that means you understand the market as well. If you don't understand your market, you'll struggle to get pricing that the market will bear and understand how to set up marketing that works.

'If you don't understand your business model, you could price yourself under what the market will bear in order to try and undercut and gain clients – and damage your profit margins and stability.

'For example, I have a client who does a phenomenal job of leveraging community relationships because they know that being present in the community really makes a massive difference in their particular market for their product.

'Others in the market don't put as much emphasis on being present in the community at events and with their marketing, and it shows.'

KNOWING YOUR PLACE IN THE MARKET

Carla Williams Johnson says that in order to understand your place in the market, you have to delve deep into what it really is that you do. This understanding, she said, goes far beyond a simple label or a job description; it speaks to the need you are trying to fulfil.

'You have to be absolutely clear on what you do and how you help people and you also have to know if there's even a market for what you're selling.

'Would people actually want to buy or do you maybe have to look at launching somewhere else?'

She adds: 'You are more than your job description or service, you are providing a solution.

'So, for example, a photographer is never just a photographer; they capture moments in time that you can relive for years and years.

'An event planner is never just an event planner; they help you create memories that will last a lifetime.

'I am not just a marketing expert; I give my clients the clarity and the confidence they need to fully implement successful strategies, so that they can make the impact and the income they desire.

'My point is this: you are more than just what you do, so understanding this will help you determine where to show up, and who to show up to, because there is someone out there who is in need of your unique combination of skills, and only you have the answer to their problems.

'Being clear on what you offer as well can help you not just attract the right people to your brand but repel the persons who are just

not a great fit. It works both ways. Knowing your market will help you determine when would be the ideal time to promote and how to position your offerings.

'You'll be able to take into consideration the public's frame of mind so that your message would be well received and know the right creative (language, visuals, tone, copy, media, etc) that should be used to effectively connect with your audience to make the messaging more appealing.

'You will also be aware of emerging trends that you can capitalize on in order to market yourself more effectively and, most importantly, understand the culture of the market you're hoping to sell in so you can integrate your brand more effectively.

'All in all, as you continue in business more and more things would be revealed to you, helping you make better choices as you move forward.'

OBSERVING THE MARKET

We have spoken before about the need to assess and observe the market and this is something that is absolutely crucial at every stage. The market is constantly changing, with new rivals entering the fray and leaving the field, as well as changes to what customers want and how they want it.

For marketing and brand expert Carla, it is all about observation, which she splits into three distinct aspects:
■ competitors;
■ trends;
■ customers.

When assessing competitors, Carla has the following advice: 'I logically observe what others do, especially the thought leaders in my industry. I study their strategies, how they interact with their customers and their execution techniques to understand why people purchase.'

CHAPTER 8

Carla says she then asks herself the following questions:
- ■ Can I utilize what they're doing in my business?
- ■ Are they leaving gaps in their service that I can now capitalize on?
- ■ Can I improve a product or service I already have – or do I create something new?
- ■ Can there be a collaboration in the future if we share the same clients?

She says that studying emerging trends in your market is also vital, as is taking note of how your target market is evolving over time.

'While some trends may be quite clear, such as an increase in shopping during the holiday season, some trends grow over time and you have to be aware of them.

'For example, here in Trinidad and Tobago it was only in the last few years that suppliers of the East Indian delicacy Roti have positioned their product as a must-have for the East Indian holidays of Arrival Day and Diwali.

'So much so, that people order weeks in advance to ensure they get it in time for the holiday. My point is: a good marketer sees opportunities when they arise and positions their products or services to suit.'

Finally, Carla says she observes her potential customers. She adds that this was especially true as things changed during the COVID-19 pandemic.

'I look at what they're doing and what media they're consuming.

'If they're on social media, I look at the types of posts they gravitate to or what type of content they engage with.

'I consider if they watch television to relax, and if so what stations or types of programmes they're drawn to and so on. This will tell me where I need to show up to connect with them better.'

YOUR STRENGTHS AND WEAKNESSES IN THE MARKET
Throughout this chapter, Sun Tzu made mention of advantage and disadvantage. Knowing the qualities of an army and the terrain meant

150

that there were some types of ground offering advantages and some that do not, depending on the resources at hand and the qualities and disposition of the forces.

Consider again the example of Starbucks. The company had traits and qualities which would have provided it with huge advantages in particular markets, such as its buying power, brand awareness, management and staffing structures. But these were of no advantage in the Australian market because of the particular quirks we mentioned above. Knowing your business and knowing your terrain means you can pick and choose how to combine the attributes of both to achieve victory, and when also to avoid defeat.

Doing so is all about awareness.

Joe Wehbe says: 'To begin with I like to ask myself a different, broader question: What's an example of a market that I can't enter?

'In theory, there are not many. It comes back to asking "Who?" rather than "How?" It's also a matter of asking "Why?"

'The great entrepreneurs venture bravely into markets and industries that they have no permission being in.

'Think Branson and airlines, but there are countless examples. In fact, it almost takes an outsider to truly reform an industry or take over a market because they have a fresh "first principles" perspective, like Einstein was famous for in physics.

'They go to these places bravely because they are needed.

'There is a problem that no one else is solving, a gap no one else is closing, and a scratch that no one else will itch.'

CONCLUSIONS

Sun Tzu spoke of terrain as different types of ground, all with different qualities that provided opportunities and challenges to the leader and their army.

In a business context, we view this as the market. In order to navigate it, you should:

■ Observe the market.
Keep an eye on trends, competitors and customers.

■ Understand your place in the market.
Ask yourself what your role is and how do you traverse the obstacles.

■ Understand your advantages or disadvantages.
You may be suited or uniquely unsuited for a market, either as a business or individual. Understanding how and why can help you to success, or help you avoid expensive defeats.

Terrain

(Sun Tzu's Original Text)

1. Sun Tzu said: We may distinguish six kinds of terrain, to wit:

   (1) Accessible ground;
   (2) entangling ground;
   (3) temporizing ground;
   (4) narrow passes;
   (5) precipitous heights;
   (6) positions at a great distance from the enemy.

2. Ground which can be freely traversed by both sides is called accessible.

3. With regard to ground of this nature, be before the enemy in occupying the raised and sunny spots, and carefully guard your line of supplies. Then you will be able to fight with advantage.

4. Ground which can be abandoned but is hard to re-occupy is called entangling.

5. From a position of this sort, if the enemy is unprepared, you may sally forth and defeat him. But if the enemy is prepared for your coming, and you fail to defeat him, then, return being impossible, disaster will ensue.

6. When the position is such that neither side will gain by making the first move, it is called temporizing ground.

7. In a position of this sort, even though the enemy should offer us an attractive bait, it will be advisable not to stir forth, but rather to retreat, thus enticing the enemy in his turn; then, when part of his army has come out, we may deliver our attack with advantage.

8. With regard to narrow passes, if you can occupy them first, let them be strongly garrisoned and await the advent of the enemy.

9. Should the army forestall you in occupying a pass, do not go after him if the pass is fully garrisoned, but only if it is weakly garrisoned.

10. With regard to precipitous heights, if you are beforehand with your adversary, you should occupy the raised and sunny spots, and there wait for him to come up.

11. If the enemy has occupied them before you, do not follow him, but retreat and try to entice him away.

12. If you are situated at a great distance from the enemy, and the strength of the two armies is equal, it is not easy to provoke a battle, and fighting will be to your disadvantage.

13. These six are the principles connected with Earth. The general who has attained a responsible post must be careful to study them.

14. Now an army is exposed to six calamities, not arising from natural causes, but from faults for which the general is responsible. These are:

(1) Flight;
(2) insubordination;
(3) collapse;
(4) ruin;
(5) disorganization;
(6) rout.

15. Other conditions being equal, if one force is hurled against another ten times its size, the result will be the flight of the former.

16. When the common soldiers are too strong and their officers too weak, the result is insubordination. When the officers are too strong and the common soldiers too weak, the result is collapse.

17. When the higher officers are angry and insubordinate, and on meeting the enemy give battle on their own account from a feeling of resentment, before the commander-in-chief can tell whether or not he is in a position to fight, the result is ruin.

18. When the general is weak and without authority; when his orders are not clear and distinct; when there are no fixed duties assigned to officers and men, and the ranks are formed in a slovenly haphazard manner, the result is utter disorganization.

19. When a general, unable to estimate the enemy's strength, allows an inferior force to engage a larger one, or hurls a weak detachment against a powerful one, and neglects to place picked soldiers in the front rank, the result must be a rout.

20. These are six ways of courting defeat, which must be carefully noted by the general who has attained a responsible post.

21. The natural formation of the country is the soldier's best ally; but a power of estimating the adversary, of controlling the forces of victory, and of shrewdly calculating difficulties, dangers and distances, constitutes the test of a great general.

22. He who knows these things, and in fighting puts his knowledge into practice, will win his battles. He who knows them not, nor practises them, will surely be defeated.

23. If fighting is sure to result in victory, then you must fight, even though the ruler forbid it; if fighting will not result in victory, then you must not fight even at the ruler's bidding.

24. The general who advances without coveting fame and retreats without fearing disgrace, whose only thought is to protect his country and do good service for his sovereign, is the jewel of the kingdom.

25. Regard your soldiers as your children, and they will follow you into the deepest valleys; look upon them as your own beloved sons, and they will stand by you even unto death.

26. If, however, you are indulgent, but unable to make your authority felt; kind-hearted, but unable to enforce your commands; and incapable, moreover, of quelling disorder: then your soldiers must be likened to spoilt children; they are useless for any practical purpose.

27. If we know that our own men are in a condition to attack, but are unaware that the enemy is not open to attack, we have gone only halfway towards victory.

28. If we know that the enemy is open to attack, but are unaware that our own men are not in a condition to attack, we have gone only halfway towards victory.

29. If we know that the enemy is open to attack, and also know our men are in a condition to attack, but are unaware that the nature of the ground makes fighting impracticable, we have still gone only halfway towards victory.

30. Hence the experienced soldier, once in motion, is never bewildered; once he has broken camp, he is never at a loss.

31. Hence the saying: If you know the enemy and know yourself, your victory will not stand in doubt; if you know Heaven and know Earth, you may make your victory complete.

CHAPTER 11

THE NINE SITUATIONS

In this chapter, Sun Tzu expanded on the issue of terrain still further and spoke about what he called 'the nine situations'. This was essentially about nine varieties of ground:

- dispersive ground;
- facile ground;
- contentious ground;
- open ground;
- ground of intersecting highways;
- serious ground;
- difficult ground;
- hemmed-in ground;
- desperate ground.

According to Sun Tzu, each type of ground required different responses from the army's commander in order to move closer to victory. These could include such tactics as plunging the army deep into enemy territory with no possibility of retreat. By doing so, he said that the army would forget its fears and, with its backs to the wall, would be better placed to strike a decisive blow for victory.

There were also occasions when he said attacks could benefit from alliances. Forming relationships with other powers could provide knowledge of the ground and the enemy, while making it easier to travel through hostile territory, something touched on in earlier chapters.

ACT 'AS IF'

In this chapter, Sun Tzu said it was important to keep antagonists in awe. In a business context, this can be likened to projecting an image of the company in such a way that potential rivals are wary of trying to encroach on its market share.

> **Hence, he does not strive to ally himself with all and sundry, nor does he foster the power of other states. He carries out his own secret designs, keeping his antagonists in awe. Thus, he is able to capture their cities and overthrow their kingdoms.**

So what does this mean for business? It could mean, for instance, having an impactful social media presence on LinkedIn, Facebook, Twitter and other social media sites, displaying examples of the company and/or owner's credentials and successes.

If the company is seen to be successful, it will be easier to attract the interest of potential allies and investors, while also warding off potential hostile threats who may otherwise smell weakness. Celebrate successes, move swiftly past your failures.

BELIEVE IN YOUR BRAND

As a marketing expert, being able to create a powerful brand awareness is something Carla has been doing for years. Perception of your brand is important if you are to project an image that will inspire – if not awe, then at least competence and ability. But as importance as perception is, so too is the reality.

Carla Williams Johnson says: 'Your brand has to stand for something and it's more than just a fancy logo or your brand's colours, but how you want people to feel and that emotional connection. It's about your brand values and how you want to be represented. It's allowing that authenticity to shine through and being unapologetic about it.

'So showcasing the things that are real to you and, of course, the clients you're wanting to serve is truly the best way to show up.

'Sometimes it may not always be pretty, but I guarantee that realness would resonate and be so relatable that people would love you even more.'

COUNCIL CHAMBER AND BOARDROOM SITUATIONS

Sun Tzu spoke in this chapter of the importance of being 'stern' in the council chamber. While it was important for the leader to accept counsel, there could be only one leader, who should be firm about projecting their goals and demands.

These days, things are a little more flexible and an entrepreneur will often have to engage their board members' expertise.

In business, Fei Yao says it is important to be authoritative while also indulging other opinions.

'A balance of both is needed. We need our stakeholders to feel heard before we make key decisions.

'If they don't feel as if they have been at least heard, they are also less likely to get fully behind any decisions being made, which doesn't make for cohesive leadership and direction.'

CONCLUSIONS

In this chapter Sun Tzu spoke of the importance of creating a persona that would leave rivals in awe. He also talked about the importance of being stern in the council chamber.

In a business context this can mean:

■ Ensure your social media and public perception is positive.
It is possible to punch above your weight by having a positive image.

■ Believe in your brand.
Authenticity matters – and if you believe it, others will too.

■ Be assertive with senior managers.
It is important to take counsel, but there is only one boss.

The Nine Situations

(Sun Tzu's Original Text)

1. Sun Tzu said: The art of war recognizes nine varieties of ground:
   (1) Dispersive ground;
   (2) facile ground;
   (3) contentious ground;
   (4) open ground;
   (5) ground of intersecting highways;
   (6) serious ground;
   (7) difficult ground;
   (8) hemmed-in ground;
   (9) desperate ground.

2. When a chieftain is fighting in his own territory, it is dispersive ground.

3. When he has penetrated into hostile territory, but to no great distance, it is facile ground.

4. Ground the possession of which imports great advantage to either side, is contentious ground.

5. Ground on which each side has liberty of movement is open ground.

6. Ground which forms the key to three contiguous states, so that he who occupies it first has most of the Empire at his command, is a ground of intersecting highways.

7. When an army has penetrated into the heart of a hostile country, leaving a number of fortified cities in its rear, it is serious ground.

8. Mountain forests, rugged steeps, marshes and fens – all country that is hard to traverse: this is difficult ground.

9. Ground which is reached through narrow gorges, and from which we can only retire by tortuous paths, so that a small number of the enemy would suffice to crush a large body of our men: this is hemmed-in ground.

10. Ground on which we can only be saved from destruction by fighting without delay, is desperate ground.

11. On dispersive ground, therefore, fight not. On facile ground, halt not. On contentious ground, attack not.

12. On open ground, do not try to block the enemy's way. On the ground of intersecting highways, join hands with your allies.

13. On serious ground, gather in plunder. In difficult ground, keep steadily on the march.

14. On hemmed-in ground, resort to stratagem. On desperate ground, fight.

15. Those who were called skilful leaders of old knew how to drive a wedge between the enemy's front and rear; to prevent co-operation between his large and small divisions; to hinder the good troops from rescuing the bad, the officers from rallying their men.

16. When the enemy's men were united, they managed to keep them in disorder.

17. When it was to their advantage, they made a forward move; when otherwise, they stopped still.

18. If asked how to cope with a great host of the enemy in orderly array and on the point of marching to the attack, I should say: 'Begin by seizing something which your opponent holds dear; then he will be amenable to your will.'

19. Rapidity is the essence of war: take advantage of the enemy's unreadiness, make your way by unexpected routes, and attack unguarded spots.

20. The following are the principles to be observed by an invading force: The further you penetrate into a country, the greater will be the solidarity of your troops, and thus the defenders will not prevail against you.

21. Make forays in fertile country in order to supply your army with food.

22. Carefully study the well-being of your men, and do not overtax them. Concentrate your energy and hoard your strength. Keep your army continually on the move, and devise unfathomable plans.

23. Throw your soldiers into positions whence there is no escape, and they will prefer death to flight. If they will face death, there is nothing they may not achieve. Officers and men alike will put forth their uttermost strength.

24. Soldiers when in desperate straits lose the sense of fear. If there is no place of refuge, they will stand firm. If they are in hostile country, they will show a stubborn front. If there is no help for it, they will fight hard.

25. Thus, without waiting to be marshalled, the soldiers will be constantly on the *qui vive*; without waiting to be asked, they will do your will; without restrictions, they will be faithful; without giving orders, they can be trusted.

26. Prohibit the taking of omens, and do away with superstitious doubts. Then, until death itself comes, no calamity need be feared.

27. If our soldiers are not overburdened with money, it is not because they have a distaste for riches; if their lives are not unduly long, it is not because they are disinclined to longevity.

28. On the day they are ordered out to battle, your soldiers may weep, those sitting up bedewing their garments, and those lying down letting the tears run down their cheeks. But let them once be brought to bay, and they will display the courage of a Chu or a Kuei.

29. The skilful tactician may be likened to the shuai-jan. Now the shuai-jan is a snake that is found in the Ch'ang mountains. Strike at its head, and you will be attacked by its tail; strike at its tail, and you will be attacked by its head; strike at its middle, and you will be attacked by head and tail both.

30. Asked if an army can be made to imitate the shuai-jan, I should answer, 'Yes'. For the men of Wu and the men of Yueh are enemies; yet if they are crossing a river in the same boat and are caught by a storm, they will come to each other's assistance just as the left hand helps the right.

31. Hence it is not enough to put one's trust in the tethering of horses, and the burying of chariot wheels in the ground.

32. The principle on which to manage an army is to set up one standard of courage which all must reach.

33. How to make the best of both strong and weak, that is a question involving the proper use of ground.

34. Thus the skilful general conducts his army just as though he were leading a single man, willy-nilly, by the hand.

35. It is the business of a general to be quiet and thus ensure secrecy; upright and just, and thus maintain order.

36. He must be able to mystify his officers and men by false reports and appearances, and thus keep them in total ignorance.

37. By altering his arrangements and changing his plans, he keeps the enemy without definite knowledge. By shifting his camp and taking circuitous routes, he prevents the enemy from anticipating his purpose.

38. At the critical moment, the leader of an army acts like one who has climbed up a height and then kicks away the ladder behind him. He carries his men deep into hostile territory before he shows his hand.

39. He burns his boats and breaks his cooking-pots; like a shepherd driving a flock of sheep, he drives his men this way and that, and nothing knows whither he is going.

40. To muster his host and bring it into danger: – this may be termed the business of the general.

41. The different measures suited to the nine varieties of ground; the expediency of aggressive or defensive tactics; and the fundamental laws of human nature: these are things that must most certainly be studied.

42. When invading hostile territory, the general principle is that penetrating deeply brings cohesion; penetrating but a short way means dispersion.

43. When you leave your own country behind, and take your army across neighbourhood territory, you find yourself on critical ground. When there are means of communication on all four sides, the ground is one of intersecting highways.

44. When you penetrate deeply into a country, it is serious ground. When you penetrate but a little way, it is facile ground.

45. When you have the enemy's strongholds in your rear, and narrow passes in front, it is hemmed-in ground. When there is no place of refuge at all, it is desperate ground.

46. Therefore, on dispersive ground, I would inspire my men with unity of purpose. On facile ground, I would see that there is close connection between all parts of my army.

47. On contentious ground, I would hurry up my rear.

48. On open ground, I would keep a vigilant eye on my defences. On ground of intersecting highways, I would consolidate my alliances.

49. On serious ground, I would try to ensure a continuous stream of supplies. On difficult ground, I would keep pushing on along the road.

50. On hemmed-in ground, I would block any way of retreat. On desperate ground, I would proclaim to my soldiers the hopelessness of saving their lives.

51. For it is the soldier's disposition to offer an obstinate resistance when surrounded, to fight hard when he cannot help himself, and to obey promptly when he has fallen into danger.

52. We cannot enter into alliance with neighbouring princes until we are acquainted with their designs. We are not fit to lead an army on the march unless we are familiar with the face of the country – its mountains and forests, its pitfalls and precipices, its marshes and swamps. We shall be unable to turn natural advantages to account unless we make use of local guides.

53. To be ignorant of any one of the following four or five principles does not befit a warlike prince.

54. When a warlike prince attacks a powerful state, his generalship shows itself in preventing the concentration of the enemy's forces. He overawes his opponents, and their allies are prevented from joining against him.

55. Hence he does not strive to ally himself with all and sundry, nor does he foster the power of other states. He carries out his own secret designs, keeping his antagonists in awe. Thus he is able to capture their cities and overthrow their kingdoms.

56. Bestow rewards without regard to rule, issue orders without regard to previous arrangements; and you will be able to handle a whole army as though you had to do with but a single man.

57. Confront your soldiers with the deed itself; never let them know your design. When the outlook is bright, bring it before their eyes; but tell them nothing when the situation is gloomy.

58. Place your army in deadly peril, and it will survive; plunge it into desperate straits, and it will come off in safety.

59. For it is precisely when a force has fallen into harm's way that it is capable of striking a blow for victory.

60. Success in warfare is gained by carefully accommodating ourselves to the enemy's purpose.

61. By persistently hanging on the enemy's flank, we shall succeed in the long run in killing the commander-in-chief.

62. This is called the ability to accomplish a thing by sheer cunning.

63. On the day that you take up your command, block the frontier passes, destroy the official tallies, and stop the passage of all emissaries.

64. Be stern in the council-chamber, so that you may control the situation.

65. If the enemy leaves a door open, you must rush in.

66. Forestall your opponent by seizing what he holds dear, and subtly contrive to time his arrival on the ground.

67. Walk in the path defined by rule, and accommodate yourself to the enemy until you can fight a decisive battle.

68. At first, then, exhibit the coyness of a maiden, until the enemy gives you an opening; afterwards emulate the rapidity of a running hare, and it will be too late for the enemy to oppose you.

CHAPTER 12

ATTACK BY FIRE

The concept of fire in Sun Tzu's era is a far-reaching one. During his era, when the only weapons available were made of steel and wood, fire represented the ultimate means of destruction. It was unwieldy, difficult to tame, and using it inappropriately could have dire consequences for the general and his army. It could be the great leveller, ripping through a camp in a way that left all battle plans, tactics, numerical troop superiority and weapons pointless.

In a business context, the idea of fire is analogous to anything that unleashes unprecedented upheaval in a market or upon a company and industry.

Just like a well-prepared army felled by a relentless and undefeatable blaze, during these types of economic and social circumstances, even huge financial reserves, skilled staff, brand loyalty and all the other tools, which would normally stand a company in a strong position to handle most situations, may not be enough.

The COVID-19 pandemic and credit crunch, for example, are relatively recent instances where chaos has engulfed entire sectors, sweeping through the global economy and leaving devastation in their wake. Household names and smaller SMEs alike went to the wall in numbers never seen before.

While these events have unleashed forces that have led tragically to the loss of millions of jobs and businesses, many companies have been able to reinvent themselves or change how they do business not only to survive, but thrive.

Examples include clothing companies that began to manufacture masks and PPE, restaurants and bars which started delivering directly to people's homes, as well as those employees who had sadly lost their jobs but who decided to begin their own entrepreneurial journeys, doing things such as setting up online businesses to serve growing new markets.

BE THE PHOENIX IN THE FLAMES

Even during the most tumultuous of times, some companies have still been able to thrive if they were able to adapt and exploit the potential opportunities on offer.

Once again this returns to our earlier point about being prepared to move when the time is right. And when that opportunity comes, be brave and decisive.

This may not be the case for every business. During the Covid pandemic and ensuing lockdowns for example, many companies faced insurmountable obstacles that were simply beyond their control, regardless of how prepared they were.

Entire sectors were forced to bolt their doors and in those situations, tragically, there is very little scope for adapting and surviving.

But in some sectors there has been some leeway to adapt, while new markets have also opened up. In the spirit of Sun Tzu, when opportunities do present themselves, it is vital to be daring and decisive in order to make the most of them.

Stephanie Scheller says: 'When the economy gets tumultuous, incredible opportunities open up for the businesses that are poised to take advantage of them.

'If you've carefully managed your business to protect your profit margins and have cash on hand, you'll set yourself up to be able to propel your business forward expansively when the crisis hits. But you also have to cultivate a mindset of expansion and growth.

'It's easy to hunker down and wait for things to pass, but the businesses that will explode on the other side (and through it) are the ones moving forward.'

AGGRESSIVE ATTACKS

Just as an army can unleash fire upon its foe, there are times when an entrepreneur may want to put aside more nuanced approaches to the market they are entering and take decisive action that is designed to make a big splash.

THE LETTINGS GAME

When Joe Wehbe's company was trying to make an impact on the Sydney lettings scene, he launched a decisive and sweeping plan of attack: the '$9,999' model, selling homes for a fixed fee of $9,999, rather than for a commission on the final sales price.

This business model drew comparisons to online estate agents Purplebricks because of the fee, but Joe's company also threw in additional services, such as making video and social media advertising more commonplace in homes – something which, he says, hardly anyone in the Australian real estate market offers. 'We are already seeing a lot of attempts at real estate service innovation, particularly out of the USA. We received a lot of criticism and scrutiny from other traditional agents, expectedly so, but one has to ask: "Do we have an obligation to customers, or to the competition?"'

Citing Uber and other rideshare disruptors, he adds: 'A line I actually heard from another Australian entrepreneur was "price is only an obstacle in the absence of value".

'The question for me comes down to intentions. Are your eyes on the customer, or the competition?

'Are you looking to create value, or win market share? Is the offer you are providing genuine, or is it based on deception?'

He adds: 'Every piece of experience and reading has taught me that for the long-term players, you win by focusing on others. In the short-term game, the reverse holds true.

'But it's hard to play both games.

'For me personally, the short-term games don't feel worthwhile, because the rewards on offer aren't particularly interesting to me.'

STAYING FOCUSED

Keeping your wits about you as things get difficult is easier said than done, but it is something Arun Kapil managed to do with Green Saffron when he launched it in 2007, right in the middle of the credit crunch.

'To a certain extent, I think that naïve blind faith was key. I just ran at things with a singular focus.

'In 2007 I was only just starting off on my market stall with Olive, a local young lady, who was helping out.'

During the COVID-19 pandemic, Arun said the challenges were very different in terms of the speed with which businesses and customers closed their doors happened literally overnight.

'It was as if falling off a cliff,' says Arun. 'At least with the credit crunch, you had an audience to whom you had a hope of making a sale.'

INNOVATE AND ADAPT

One of the many benefits entrepreneurs have over larger companies is the ability to be fleet of foot, and this can be a huge boon during times of extreme market duress. Unlike larger corporations, SMEs can change course quickly when the need arises, abandoning old business ideas and crafting new ones quickly if they have to.

And according to Arun, navigating the choppy waters of those early days in 2007 was all about one word: innovation.

'The business had one core revenue stream when we started, that quickly grew to two streams; our market stalls and local retail outlets.

'On a market stall, I believe the key to success is to consistently attract new customers with an ever-evolving range of products whilst maintaining your core offering.'

Indeed, Saasha Celestial-One's continued success as a disruptor with Olio has very much involved an acceptance that the only certainty for a start-up is that nothing is certain.

'The only thing that is certain is that things are always changing!

'Our philosophy is to always be experimenting. Ben Horowitz, the famous venture capital investor, says in his book *The Hard Thing About Hard Things* that start-ups should be innovating ten times a day – and it's this relentless pace of innovation that keeps the wind in the sales of a start-up.

'Of course, very few of these experiments/innovations will work, but you won't know until you try!'

DIVERSIFY YOUR OFFERING

Challenging times close doors, but they also open new ones too. Diversifying where revenue comes from is a crucial weapon in any entrepreneur's armoury.

Arun says: 'We now have three core revenue streams, which we refer to as pillars, or business units if you will.

'In essence the theory is the same, just the delivery is different. Online sales were not a thing in 2007. This year, Pillar One, our ad hoc demand stream which includes our farmers' markets, was all about pivoting to a delivery service, online sales and the launch of new products such as our "Curry In A Box" delivered meal kits.'

ADAPT TO SURVIVE

The COVID-19 pandemic caused economic chaos right around the world, requiring companies to be swift and decisive if they were going to be able to deal with the fallout. Having launched and thrived during the credit crunch, Arun and his team once again found themselves having to think on their feet.

'We launched new products more fit for (COVID) purpose, pivoted the business to realign its focus and followed the HSE (Health and Safety Executive) and WHO (World Health Organization) guidance to the letter.

'Most importantly, we also took up the wage subsidy scheme.

'This was a lifesaver. Once our staff jobs were secure, we could take a breath to assess what to do.

'I'm really proud of our team and how we all pulled together, getting stuck into whatever was needed to be done.

'Probably the biggest benefit our business has gleaned from this most unprecedented of times is completing its three-year strategic plan.

'We were on a track to reorganize the business infrastructure – its core model, if you will.

'This pandemic has, rather bizarrely allowed us the time to plan more thoroughly, take a much-needed breath and to refocus. Time will tell if we're right.'

HOPE FOR THE BEST, PREPARE FOR THE WORST

You can never be fully prepared for the kind of devastation that has resulted from events such as COVID-19, but there are mitigation measures a business can put in place. So as someone who has been through two turbulent events with his business, what would be Arun's most important piece of advice?

'Plan, plan, plan and be prepared to adapt at the drop of a hat.

'Easy words to write, but I absolutely believe the more agile you remain, the better.

'It's … a state of mind more than anything. Once you become stuck in a rut, content with a certain way of doing things, you're liable to miss opportunities. Stay feisty, work collaboratively and listen to those you trust.'

CONCLUSIONS

In this chapter Sun Tzu spoke about attacking by fire. It could have a hugely destructive influence and lay waste to whole areas, but it could also be used as a tactical weapon to achieve an advantage.

In the context of business then, we conclude:

■ Doing something hugely disruptive to a market can bring success.

■ Financial disasters happen and you can prepare for them.

■ Difficult times breed invention and innovation.

Attack by Fire

(Sun Tzu's Original Text)

1. Sun Tzu said: There are five ways of attacking with fire. The first is to burn soldiers in their camp; the second is to burn stores; the third is to burn baggage trains; the fourth is to burn arsenals and magazines; the fifth is to hurl dropping fire amongst the enemy.

2. In order to carry out an attack, we must have means available. The material for raising fire should always be kept in readiness.

3. There is a proper season for making attacks with fire, and special days for starting a conflagration.

4. The proper season is when the weather is very dry; the special days are those when the moon is in the constellations of the Sieve, the Wall, the Wing or the Cross-bar; for these four are all days of rising wind.

5. In attacking with fire, one should be prepared to meet five possible developments:

6. (1) When fire breaks out inside the enemy's camp, respond at once with an attack from without.

7. (2) If there is an outbreak of fire, but the enemy's soldiers remain quiet, bide your time and do not attack.

8. (3) When the force of the flames has reached its height, follow it up with an attack, if that is practicable; if not, stay where you are.

9. (4) If it is possible to make an assault with fire from without, do not wait for it to break out within, but deliver your attack at a favourable moment.

10. (5) When you start a fire, be to windward of it. Do not attack from the leeward.

11. A wind that rises in the daytime lasts long, but a night breeze soon falls.

12. In every army, the five developments connected with fire must be known, the movements of the stars calculated, and a watch kept for the proper days.

13. Hence those who use fire as an aid to the attack show intelligence; those who use water as an aid to the attack gain an accession of strength.

14. By means of water, an enemy may be intercepted, but not robbed of all his belongings.

15. Unhappy is the fate of one who tries to win his battles and succeed in his attacks without cultivating the spirit of enterprise; for the result is waste of time and general stagnation.

16. Hence the saying: The enlightened ruler lays his plans well ahead; the good general cultivates his resources.

17. Move not unless you see an advantage; use not your troops unless there is something to be gained; fight not unless the position is critical.

18. No ruler should put troops into the field merely to gratify his own spleen; no general should fight a battle simply out of pique.

19. If it is to your advantage, make a forward move; if not, stay where you are.

20. Anger may in time change to gladness; vexation may be succeeded by content.

21. But a kingdom that has once been destroyed can never come again into being; nor can the dead ever be brought back to life.

22. Hence the enlightened ruler is heedful, and the good general full of caution. This is the way to keep a country at peace and an army intact.

CHAPTER 13

THE USE OF SPIES

As mentioned throughout the book, Sun Tzu was an unconventional commander. He eschewed glory and bravado in favour of pragmatism. For him, proper planning meant a commander should not even have to fight at all and waste lives, land and cities.

One of his principal non-battlefield weapons in this endeavour was intelligence, and in this chapter, he spoke about the clever use of spies to gather knowledge about the enemy.

Now, while the term 'spies' does not initially lend itself to a business audience (industrial espionage is a crime!), the building of intelligence is a vital part of any company's success. We have spoken earlier in the book about gaining information about the market and opponents, and the importance of doing so and making it an ongoing endeavour simply can not be overstated.

Understanding the market you are moving into or your existing customers, becoming familiar with the competition and what their strengths and weaknesses are, are all potentially vital to success.

CUSTOMER INTELLIGENCE

When it comes to building intelligence, it should always start with what is closest to home – existing customers.

Existing customers are a gold mine because by understanding what drives them, you can better understand not only how to increase their loyalty to your brand, product or service, but it will also enable you to attract more customers too.

At a micro level, this can include simple measures such as mailshots and e-mail campaigns. You can include questionnaires that enable you to gather information, ranging from their spending priorities for the coming year to how likely they are to do their business with a rival company – and why.

Jeremy Stern said he invests far more time in understanding his customers than he does in the opposition.

'I would much rather spend time analyzing my clients, looking at their accounts, their strategic statements and working out where they are going, than at my competitors.

'The reason is simple: ignorance, not a rival, is my biggest issue.'

UNDERSTANDING YOUR RIVALS

There are, though, times when it makes sense to understand what rivals in your marketplace are doing. Not only can it help you refine your own offerings, it can also ensure you stay ahead of the curve.

Building intelligence on rival companies sounds tricky, but it can still be done in ways that are within both the boundaries of law and ethics.

Most companies will be fairly open online and on social media about how they are conducting their businesses, while rival CEOs may also publish thought-leadership pieces on LinkedIn and other platforms, and these may give an indication of their priorities.

Company accounts are also usually legally available online, which can give an indication of how rivals are performing.

While it makes sense to understand what your rivals are up to, it should not be something you obsess about or which may cause you to change too much how you go about your own business.

Fei Yao says: 'We balance keeping a close eye on competitors without obsessing over them.

'Understanding where the landscape and market is critical to drawing your own path, but there will always be another way.

'Focusing on yourself, your user feedback and your customers, and building the best product is what can ultimately guide you to success and winning the market as opposed to obsessing over competitor strategies.'

OUTSIDE EXPERTS

Sun Tzu wrote about the concept of local spies – that is, people who understood the nuances of a terrain into which the commander and their army were moving. In the business world, we can view this as the use of outside experts such as contractors.

These are people we may temporarily employ for the very reason that they bring with them existing knowledge and do not usually need to be trained or educated in that new market or way of doing things.

When hiring contractors with industry-specific expertise, be mindful that you're paying not only for their skills, but also for their knowledge of that industry too.

Joe Wehbe says: 'Enlisting the help of experts is essential, not just when moving into a different phase of one's business but in general. Sir Isaac Newton said it best when he said: "... if I have seen further than others it is by standing on the shoulders of giants."

'One can go very far simply by standing on the shoulders of giants.

'A room of experts can accomplish a great deal, but what I've found is that, whilst all these individuals are busy being experts, someone has to create the room. Someone has to bring them together.'

ACCESSING EXPERTISE

This additional market knowledge does not always have to be found via an employer–employee arrangement either; it can be accessed via networks either local or online.

Joe says: 'It is easier now than ever before to access leverage to do things, to work collaboratively with a wider range of people thanks to social media, professional networks, online communities, the internet, freelancer platforms, democratisation of media and information and more.'

In order to access that expertise, Joe again returns to his previous advice. Being sincere and being honest.

'What's the best way to find the right people to deal with? Well, the simplest answer for me is that the best way to open a thousand doors for you is to concentrate on opening doors for others.

'The people that play this game are the right kind of people, they're interested in positive-sum, long-term games.

'It's something I observed with famous authors when I was researching book publishing and marketing.

'The right relationships to leverage are not built overnight but take time and generosity to cultivate.'

SPOTTING THE RIGHT PEOPLE TO HELP YOU

When hiring outside experts and consultants, Joe says he has found the following helpful:

'People who communicate clearly and promptly as a rule of thumb offer a good service. Experts or consultants who ask very thought-provoking or challenging questions are almost always well considered in my experience.

'If they get to the heart of not what you're doing but why you're doing it, it's a good sign. Also, they make you feel like you understand.

'You'd expect the best university lecturers to wield a heavy vocabulary and be hard to decipher, but that couldn't be further from the truth.

'The best experts lack ego, and as such, they make you feel like you understand complicated things. This builds huge trust and is something to look for.'

TAKE TIME TO APPOINT THE RIGHT EXPERT

Brand expert Carla Williams Johnson says that there are times when bringing in an outside expert can be a good idea – but advises that it still makes sense to tread carefully.

'It is so very important to have the right team and I am a firm believer in investing in the help that you need in order to take your business further.

'I completely understand the process of alleviating the concerns that come with choosing the right someone to build a business.

'I get that it's not just about promising to get the job done or being the best creatively, it's something so much more. And the lesson I learned is that trusting anyone with your most prized possession (your brand's image) can make you feel a bit worrisome, so firstly, begin by considering the reason for your search; this will help you narrow your choices to determine the best fit.'

CONCLUSIONS

Sun Tzu taught of the importance of using spies to gain intelligence on both the enemy, and the terrain.

From a business point of view, this can mean:

■ Gather information on your customers.
Mail shots, surveys, etc, will help you understand their needs.

■ Understand your rivals.
Check out their social media and even their company accounts to build a picture of how they are doing.

■ Employ experts if needed.
You can use contractors and consultants who understand the nuances of particular markets, but do not be afraid to leverage free networks and existing connections too.

The Use of Spies

(Sun Tzu's Original Text)

1. Sun Tzu said: Raising a host of a hundred thousand men and marching them great distances entails heavy loss on the people and a drain on the resources of the State. The daily expenditure will amount to a thousand ounces of silver. There will be commotion at home and abroad, and men will drop down exhausted on the highways. As many as seven hundred thousand families will be impeded in their labour.

2. Hostile armies may face each other for years, striving for the victory which is decided in a single day. This being so, to remain in ignorance of the enemy's condition simply because one grudges the outlay of a hundred ounces of silver in honours and emoluments is the height of inhumanity.

3. One who acts thus is no leader of men, no present help to his sovereign, no master of victory.

4. Thus, what enables the wise sovereign and the good general to strike and conquer, and achieve things beyond the reach of ordinary men, is foreknowledge.

5. Now this foreknowledge cannot be elicited from spirits; it cannot be obtained inductively from experience, nor by any deductive calculation.

6. Knowledge of the enemy's dispositions can only be obtained from other men.

7. Hence the use of spies, of whom there are five classes:
   (1) Local spies;
   (2) inward spies;
   (3) converted spies;
   (4) doomed spies;
   (5) surviving spies.

8. When these five kinds of spy are all at work, none can discover the secret system. This is called 'divine manipulation of the threads'. It is the sovereign's most precious faculty.

9. Having local spies means employing the services of the inhabitants of a district.

10. Having inward spies, means making use of officials of the enemy.

11. Having converted spies, means getting hold of the enemy's spies and using them for our own purposes.

12. Having doomed spies, doing certain things openly for purposes of deception, and allowing our spies to know of them and report them to the enemy.

13. Surviving spies, finally, are those who bring back news from the enemy's camp.

14. Hence it is that with none in the whole army are more intimate relations to be maintained than with spies. None should be more liberally rewarded. In no other business should greater secrecy be preserved.

15. Spies cannot be usefully employed without a certain intuitive sagacity.

16. They cannot be properly managed without benevolence and straightforwardness.

17. Without subtle ingenuity of mind, one cannot make certain of the truth of their reports.

18. Be subtle! be subtle! and use your spies for every kind of business.

19. If a secret piece of news is divulged by a spy before the time is ripe, he must be put to death together with the man to whom the secret was told.

20. Whether the object be to crush an army, to storm a city, or to assassinate an individual, it is always necessary to begin by finding out the names of the attendants, the aides-de-camp, and door-keepers and sentries of the general in command. Our spies must be commissioned to ascertain these.

21. The enemy's spies who have come to spy on us must be sought out, tempted with bribes, led away and comfortably housed. Thus they will become converted spies and available for our service.

22. It is through the information brought by the converted spy that we are able to acquire and employ local and inward spies.

23. It is owing to his information, again, that we can cause the doomed spy to carry false tidings to the enemy.

24. Lastly, it is by his information that the surviving spy can be used on appointed occasions.

25. The end and aim of spying in all its five varieties is knowledge of the enemy; and this knowledge can only be derived, in the first instance, from the converted spy. Hence it is essential that the converted spy be treated with the utmost liberality.

26. Of old, the rise of the Yin dynasty was due to I Chih who had served under the Hsia. Likewise, the rise of the Chou dynasty was due to Lu Ya who had served under the Yin.

27. Hence it is only the enlightened ruler and the wise general who will use the highest intelligence of the army for purposes of spying and thereby they achieve great results. Spies are a most important element in warfare, because on them depends an army's ability to move.